Crackle Glass Too:
1950s -2000

Leslie Piña

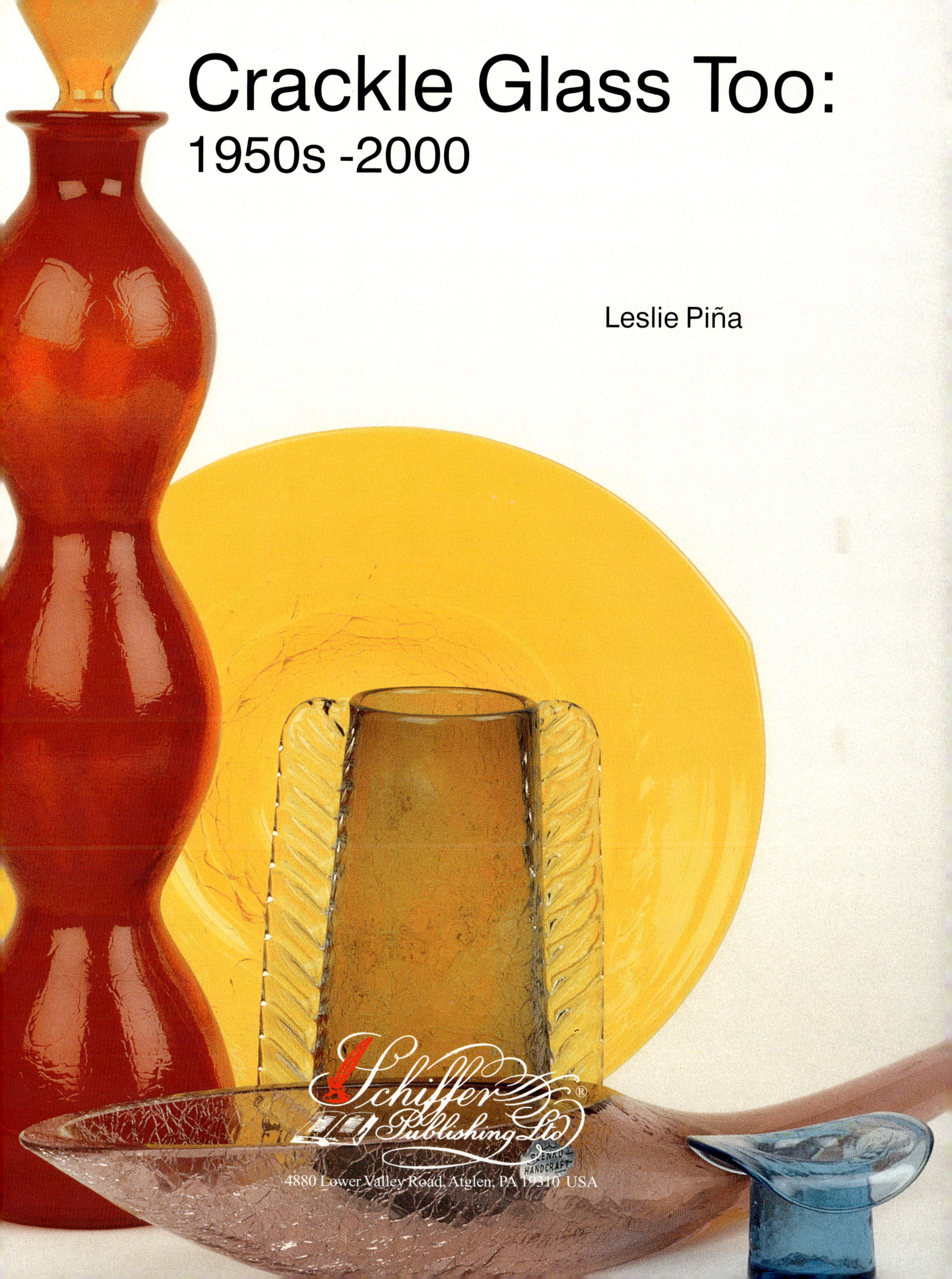

Schiffer Publishing Ltd
4880 Lower Valley Road, Atglen, PA 19310 USA

Acknowledgments

Without Aimee Bolt's extraordinary enthusiasm and dedication, this collection of crackle glass would not have been assembled. Many thanks to Aimee and her husband Wayne for their hospitality and invaluable assistance while photographing all of the pieces in this book. Aimee also assisted with research and wrote the foreword, for which I am grateful. Thanks also to our mutual friend, glassworker, and collector, Robert McKeand for valuable information he generously shared with us.

Ramón, my partner with photography and in life, knows how much he is needed. My friends at Schiffer, Doug Congdon-Martin, Peter, and Nancy should know how much I appreciate them too. Thank you all.

Library of Congress Card Number: 2001089993

Designed by Leslie Piña
Layout by Bonnie M. Hensley
Type set in Swis721 BT

ISBN: 0-7643-1404-1
Printed in Hong Kong
1 2 3 4

Published by Schiffer Publishing Ltd.
4880 Lower Valley Road
Atglen, PA 19310
Phone: (610) 593-1777; Fax: (610) 593-2002
E-mail: Schifferbk@aol.com
Please visit our web site catalog at
www.schifferbooks.com
We are always looking for people to write books on new and related subjects. If you have an idea for a book please contact us at the above address.

This book may be purchased from the publisher.
Include $3.95 for shipping.
Please try your bookstore first.
You may write for a free catalog.

In Europe, Schiffer books are distributed by
Bushwood Books
6 Marksbury Ave.
Kew Gardens
Surrey TW9 4JF England
Phone: 44 (0) 20 8392-8585; Fax: 44 (0) 20 8392-9876
E-mail: Bushwd@aol.com
Free postage in the U.K., Europe; air mail at cost.

Contents

Foreword:
Aimee Bolt 4

Introduction 5
Companies 7

Chapter One: Stoppers 16
Decanters 16
Cruets 46

Chapter Two: Vases 60

Chapter Three: Handles 81

Chapter Four: Beverage Sets & Tableware 108

Chapter Five: Bowls & Baskets 123

Chapter Six: Lighting & Figurals 143

Bibliography 157

Index 158

Foreword

Aimee Bolt

I discovered my first piece of West Virginia crackle glass in 1992 at a local antique market in Bloomington, Illinois. At the time, I wanted to start a collection of amethyst (purple) glass, and my first piece happened to be a Pilgrim #764 miniature Amethyst pitcher. I found another piece of crackle glass at the next table—Pilgrim #765 miniature Olive Green pitcher. With those two purchases, my original plan to collect amethyst changed to the quest for crackle. At first, I focused on miniature pitchers, but I soon discovered larger pitchers, baskets, bowls, decanters, vases, fruit, fish, and other fascinating pieces.

As my personal collection grew, I needed to learn about the glass—where it came from, who produced it, and how it was made. In 1992 I could find little of this information in books. After speaking with a local antiques appraiser, I learned that most of it was produced in West Virginia. I was also given the number to contact the Pilgrim Glass Corp. in Ceredo, West Virginia. My call to Pilgrim was warmly received, and I was given the name and phone number of a then 35-year employee, Robert G. McKeand. Within a few months my fiance (now husband) and I drove to West Virginia to meet Mr. McKeand and begin learning about crackle glass.

Mr. McKeand generously loaned me various company catalogs—Pilgrim, Bischoff, Kanawha, Rainbow—to start my lessons in crackle glass identification. From then on I have been also collecting books, articles, catalogs, and other information about the companies and the glass that now fills my collection and the pages of this book.

As collectors face a new decade, century, and millennium, there is an urgency to accurately identify pieces of West Virginia crackle glass produced in the twentieth century. Many join me in my belief that some of the finest crackle glass produced has come from the hands of the skilled craftsmen of West Virginia. My heartfelt thanks goes to all of them for their hard work and dedication in providing us with this beautiful, decorative, and often unusual glassware.

My collection would not be what it is today if not for some very special dealers in Illinois and Missouri who have helped me find and acquire some extraordinary pieces of crackle glass: Bill and Sheila Siebenthal; Ralph and Doris DeVore; Robert and Brigitte Aten; Antonio and Julie Donku; Peter and Joanne Krus; Charlie and Peggy Childs; and James Gibson Jr., plus Ebay sellers Anna and Jesse Wellman; Gale Ferguson; Art and Cathy Dion; Bruce Halewa; Lora Black; Hansel Jividen; Ken and Ann Van De Veer; and Larry and Barb Smuckler.

I would also like to thank some special people who have encouraged me to pursue my passion and dreams: my husband, Wayne; my mother, Margery Desnoyers; my childhood friend and best friend now, Amy Filerman; and my dear friends Earl and Delores Kopp and Christine DeBolt. Last but by no means least, I thank Robert G. McKeand of the Pilgrim Glass Corp. for his kindness in answering my endless questions and for our many conversations; Matt Carter, designer for Blenko Glass Co. for the personal tour he gave my husband and me in the summer of 1999, which included the creation of a memorable crackle glass fish. I would also like to thank Dr. Leslie Piña for the exclusivity she gave my collection in this book.

Introduction

Crackle is a finish added to the hot glass to give it an overall cracked or crackled texture. This finish affects neither the color nor the form of the piece. Nor is it associated with any particular style or company. In fact, many designs, such as by Blenko, could be ordered in either plain or crackle finish (crackle is designated by a C or a * in the catalogs). The crackle finish is added by immersing the piece in cold water while it is still hot. Sudden and extreme change in temperature shocks the glass and causes it to crack. It is then reheated to smooth and strengthen it, leaving irregular lines of crackling. The size and fineness of these lines varies from company to company and can itself become an identifying feature.

Because collectors of crackle glass focus on this special finish, collections are widely varied—from miniatures or "window" pieces in traditional forms, to big modern designer pieces. Generally, the small common examples command very reasonable prices, even though they are usually mouth-blown and handmade. On the high end of the range are the Blenko pieces from the '50s and '60s that are sought after by other collectors. Mid-century modern enthusiasts often accessorize with these large, bold, brilliantly colored pieces. And as might be expected, many of these designer pieces were copied (both carefully and badly) by several of the contemporary glass factories. It is this category of direct copies and close imitations that can be challenging to the collector. Attribution can be almost impossible if the copy is good, but there is usually some qualitative difference in addition to overall appearance. By direct comparison, the original design will usually stand apart.

Dozens of companies made crackle glass at one time or another, but during the years from about the 1940s to the 1970s, West Virginia companies produced the majority of all crackle glass on the market today. Blenko, Pilgrim, Rainbow, Bischoff, and Kanawha (and to a lesser extent, Viking) were responsible for most of the colorful crackle glass seen at flea markets, shows, shops, malls, and on the internet. Other companies like Hamon, Gibson, Empire, Heritage, and Blue Del made crackle glass, but without labels or published catalogs, these can be difficult to identify.

Color can often aid in identifying pieces, because the carefully guarded formulas for specific colors were used consistently over the years. However names of colors can be confusing. For example, Blenko's popular amberina was called Tangerine. Other companies made amberina and also used the name Tangerine—but not necessarily in the same way. The name Tangerine might mean amberina, as it does for Blenko, and it might mean solid orange. Amber, another popular color, goes under several names—from Golden Amber to Honey or Wheat, depending on whether it is a dark or light tone. If a company named a color and used it in its catalogs, the name has been capitalized in the following captions. If the name is generic or not known to be official, it is lower case in the captions. Rather than confuse collectors, this should help the reader become more familiar with specific company colors and aid in identification based on color.

Sometimes the form or even the size of an item can help identify the company. Generally, the majority of the miniature vases, pitchers, and jugs were made by Pilgrim and Rainbow. Blenko made very few lines of miniatures, and these were usually little versions of regular-sized items in the line. These modern shapes are among the easiest to identify of all the miniatures. Others, such as by Rainbow, Pilgrim, or Kanawha can be confused with each other. Bischoff copies muddy the water further.

Most extremely large stoppered bottles, pitchers, and unique designs were designed by Wayne Husted from 1952 to 1962. Distinguishable from both Blenko's early tableware designs and the modern forms introduced by their first in-house designer, Winslow Anderson (designed 1946 to 1952 and less known for crackle), these Husted pieces have given Blenko its reputation as the leading producer of big, colorful fifties glass. He was succeeded in 1963 by Joel Myers, who followed Husted's lead plus introduced other memorable modern designs. Few of these outstanding designs were attempted by other companies, with the exception of Pilgrim designs by the Moretti brothers, Alessandro and Roberto. But Moretti designs introduced Murano style to Pilgrim rather than items suitable for crackle.

Blenko models that were widely copied include the pinched ivy vases, a variety of pitchers, early stoppered bottles, and Anderson's bent-neck decanter. The other companies also introduced lines made to compete with, rather than copy, Blenko. Pilgrim had lines with satin finish, peachblow coloration, speckles, Murano-styled animal figurines, and heavy cased pieces. Kanawha, usually distinguishable by its traditional forms and a molded foot rather than a pontil mark, also made cased items with white interiors and bright exteriors. Besides their blatant knock-offs, Bischoff produced some of the most bizarre forms of all. But all of these West Virginia companies were responsible for the crackle glass made during the mid-century decades that fascinates collectors. Those still in business, notably Blenko and Pilgrim, still produce crackle glass. It can be easily distinguished from other new crackle glass—from the cheap molded items made in China and other countries to one-of-a-kind studio pieces.

With increased interest in vintage crackle, prices have risen, sometimes dramatically. Rather than rely on prices from various publications or asking prices form sales sources, I have focused more on actual selling prices in compiling the value guide. For example, although miniatures have been valued much higher by some, they normally sell in a modest range. Size is very important—the bigger the better, according to most collectors. Generic pieces with no particular designer or even company attribution also command lower prices than comparable items that can be identified. Labels are desirable, but they should not be relied upon too heavily; paper labels are very easy to transfer. Relative rarity will affect price, perhaps more than other criteria. Some of Husted's designs for Blenko, for example, were produced for a very short time. Conversely, some early (1930s or 1940s) Blenko designs remained in the line for decades and are common today. A common piece, even of quality design and craftsmanship, will be less valuable than a rare item. Some of the least common designs were unusual forms that were more costly to produce. These also happen to be among the most collectible, because of both rarity and fascination with the unusual. Some colors are more costly to produce. Generally, the earth tones and duller colors—ambers, browns, dull greens, grays—will command prices at the lower end of the range. Rich clear spectrum colors—red, orange yellow, green, blue, purple—are usually at the high end of the range. Unusual colors—Blenko's Rosé and Charcoal, cranberry, clear amethyst—may command a premium.

Prices for crackle glass vary widely and change quickly, so this can only be a guide. Its purpose is simply to help distinguish between the desirable and the less desirable pieces, and give as close an estimate of valuable as is possible at this writing. *Neither the author nor the publisher can be responsible for any outcomes from consulting this guide.* Both, however, wish you luck in the chase and enjoyment with the find.

Unidentified crackle.

Blenko crackle in catalog 2000: #9623 Cobalt vase. 9-1/2" h. #882 Azure apple. 4" h. #2015 Emerald Green decanter. 12" h.

Blenko label 2000.

Blenko label 2000.

Blenko

Blenko Glass Co., along the Mud River running through Milton, West Virginia, began by making stained glass for windows. Although today it is better known for colorful oversized bottles and an assortment of decorative items, Blenko still rolls out flat glass from large cylinders and remains the major American producer of "antique" stained glass for architectural installations.

When William John Blenko (1855-1933) left London in 1893, his goal was to make and market handmade stained glass in the United States. At that time only machine-made "cathedral" glass was being made in the United States, while handmade glass was imported from Europe. Blenko believed that he could place quality over quantity and make a niche for himself by offering antique stained glass in the United States at competitive prices.

After several failures, and at age sixty-seven, a weary Blenko made a final try, at Milton, West Virginia, calling his modest plant Eureka Glass Company. Blenko tried to persuade his younger son, William H., to join him, but aside from financial help from William and his brother, Walter, the elder Blenko was in it alone. The next year however, in 1923, William H. (Bill) joined his father in Milton. As if Blenko hadn't had enough trouble, the Crash of 1929 had a profound effect on stained glass usage. Bill's idea to expand into decorative wares—vases, bottles, and the like—proved to be both a quick fix and the first step toward later success. Blenko's considerable knowledge of chemistry and experience with formulating colors could be applied to the new line of decorative wares.

Two Swedish-American glassworkers from the Huntington Tumbler Co., Louis and Axel Muller, agreed to work at Blenko part-time in the evenings. Their skills at glassmaking and at teaching local workers proved invaluable. Now that Blenko had the idea, the facilities, and the skills in place, he needed a mechanism for marketing. A German immigrant by the name of Eddie Rubel had a talent for sales and a New York based company called Rubel and Fenton. Rubel was the perfect choice for an agent, especially since New York was the critical location for distribution, but Blenko had other representatives such as Robert Pierce in Chicago and Reginald Markham in Texas and California.

Decorative wares attracted consumers, and major department and specialty stores featured them. Crackle finish was an option on some of these popular Blenko designs—designated by the letter "C" in the model number. Both large and small crackle were used, so Blenko crackle items are identified in the same way as plain Blenko—by form and by color. Although crackle glass doesn't appear in the catalog until 1946, it was probably made a little earlier, especially on their popular lines with applied leaves or rosettes.

The only Blenko pieces that might be difficult to identify are closely copied designs, such as Anderson's bent-neck decanter. Most Blenko crackle is easy to identify, especially if it appears in catalogs. A number of these catalogs are readily available, because they have been reprinted. Miniatures, generally the most troublesome crackle items to identify, are easy to attribute to Blenko. The company produced very few miniatures and those were in modern shapes mimicking their full-sized counterparts. But the most impressive and collectible crackle pieces are the larger vases, pitchers, and decanters—the designer pieces by the fifties and sixties trio of Winslow Anderson (1946-1952), Wayne Husted (1952-1963), and Joel Myers (1963-1970). During the 1970s and 1980s, Blenko designers John Nickerson (1970-1975) and Don Shepherd (1975-1988) often used old design molds as the basis for new designs. In addition to these more economical, though less inspired, models, the designers also introduced original designs, which have already joined the ranks of the Blenko mid-century classics. Blenko continued to produce off-hand glass under the direction of Hank Adams (1988-94), Chris Gibbons (1994-1995), and Matt Carter (1995 to present). Crackle glass is still being made in both crystal with applied decoration and colors.

Blenko colors include: Amethyst, Antique Green, Aqua, Azure, Charcoal, Chestnut, Cobalt Crystal, Desert Green, Ebony, Emerald, Grass, Honey, Jonquil, Kiwi, Lemon, Lilac, Nile, Olive, Orchid, Peacock, Persian, Pine, Plum, Rosé, Ruby, Sapphire, Sea Green, Sky Blue, Surf Green, Tangerine (amberina), Teal, Topaz, Turquoise, Violet, and Wheat.

Bischoff

A.F. Bischoff Glass Co. was founded by Anthony F. Bischoff in Huntington, West, Virginia in 1922. The company moved to Hurricane, West Virginia and again to Culloden, West Virginia, where it produced crackle glass from 1942 to 1963. Bischoff made items very similar to those of other West Virginian companies. In addition to using some unusual, even bizarre, original shapes, Bischoff copied designs from leaders like Blenko. Copying, an undeniably common practice, has been responsible for a great deal of confusion in identifying and dating both crackle and plain blown glass of this period. Although each company had distinctive items (Blenko certainly contributed the greatest number of original designs), many shapes were imitations of what was seen elsewhere. Some of these copies were well-executed and looked very good—perhaps just as good or even better than the originals. Since a considerable amount of skill and effort is involved in executing both a knock-off and an original design, it is curious that more originals were not made. For example, a version of the pinched #39 ivy vase, introduced in 1939 by Blenko, was also produced by several other companies. The shape is a simple one and could easily have been modified by its imitators. Yet in most cases, they chose to make the same shape. And where Blenko may not have copied neighboring companies, there is an unmistakable similarity between many of their designs and those made in Murano, Italy at the same time. However, the influence could have flowed in more than one direction.

Lancaster Colony, of Columbus, Ohio, purchased Bischoff in 1963, keeping the Bischoff name and molds. (Blenko's fifties glass designer, Wayne Husted, joined Lancaster in that year to head its design and production department.) The following year, 1964, Sloan Glass bought Bischoff, and Sloan closed in 1996.

Many of the Bischoff items bear a striking resemblance to Blenko designs, though they are sometimes modified enough to prevent confusion. Bischoff's #720 bamboo-like shape was undoubtedly inspired by Husted's design from the 1950s; but it is quite different. Similarly, neither Bischoff's #906 gurgle bottle nor #591 bent-neck model would be confused with Blenko designs—Husted's gurgle decanter or Anderson's famous bent-neck decanter (both of which were also copied by Pilgrim). The punch set, another Blenko copy, differs enough in color and form to identify it as Bischoff. But other items are more direct copies; the #328 small jug, the #900 large jug, and the #411 dented vase would be more difficult to attribute without a label.

Of course not all Bischoff designs are unoriginal. In fact, many can be recognized by a distinct style that these designs seem to share. Exaggerated forms, complicated ruffles, bumps, and baubles, crystal stoppers and handles, and generally heavier look seem to characterize the company's product. Novelty rather than modern design seems to have been the focus.

Bischoff colors include: Amberina, Amethyst, Charcoal, Copperette, Crystal, Emerald Green, Gold, Lemon, Lime, Orange, Peacock Blue, Poinsettia Red, and Wisteria.

Bischoff #8661G Gold 18-1/2" jug shown with #M-11 Peacock Blue 4-1/2". miniature.

Blue Del

Blue Del was located on 10th Street and Eighth Avenue in Huntington. The factory was in production from 1940 to 1950, when it was destroyed by a fire.

Gibson

Charles Gibson, a native of Milton, West Virginia, owns and operates Gibson Glass in Milton. He began his glass career at the former A.F. Bischoff Glass Co. and worked for Blenko for ten years. In addition to his West Virginia experience, Gibson worked for the Indiana Glass Co. and St. Clair Glass, both in Indiana, and at Ohio's Tiffin Glass Co.

Gibson Glass opened in 1976, but closed the following year when Charles Gibson returned to his calling as a Baptist preacher. He reopened the business in 1983, and today it continues to operate as a family business. His son, Phillip Gibson, is a master glassblower, and his daughter, Sharolyn Scites, works in the gift shop. Glass artist John Desmeules specializes in paperweights, and Kathy Sponsler does decorative painting on some of the glass.

Some Gibson colors include: amethyst, blue, cobalt, crystal, green, ruby, tangerine, and vaseline.

Hamon

Robert Hamon founded Hamon Glass in 1932 in Scott Depot, West Virginia, where it continues operating today. The company produced crackle glass from the late 1940s until the mid-1970s. In 1966 Hamon merged with Kanawha Glass Co. and, although the production was separate, Hamon items were included in the Kanawha catalog.

Features which help to identify a piece as Hamon include the handles and the crackle finish. The "pulled back" handles will have a ridge across the end on most Hamon crackle pieces. Like Pilgrim's style of crackle, the Hamon finish is extremely fine. This easily identifiable finish is also called "onion crackle" or "Swedish crackle."

Hamon colors include: amber, amberina, amethyst, blue, crystal, green, ruby, and smoke.

Heritage

The Heritage Glass Co. product can often be identified by its weight. They produced a thick and heavy crackle glass similar to Bischoff. Heritage items also may have an extra base, which was also crackled and bore a pontil scar. Some Heritage pitchers can be identified by a drooped spout and/or a flat "pulled back" handle.

Kanawha

When Dunbar Glass Co. in Dunbar, West Virginia closed in 1953, production head D.P. Merritt and others joined to form the Kanawha Glass Specialties Co. Named after a nearby river, the Kanawha, the company opened in 1955 and made blown crystal in addition to cutting and decorating purchased glass. In 1957 they changed the name to Kanawha Glass Company. By 1960 they began production of the colorful decorative wares that have become so familiar, especially crackle glass. Soon Kanawha was making 350 production items in seven colors.

In 1969 Kanawha purchased Hamon Handcrafted Glass in Scott Depot, West Virginia. Hamon had begun in 1932, and their crackle glass production during the 1950s and 1960s coincided with that of other companies. The Hamon crackle glass that was added to the Kanawha line retained its identity, which explains why Kanawha catalogs often show two different types of glass—molded and hand blown.

In the early 1970s, cased milk glass was introduced in which the outer (or sometimes inner) layer was made in bright solid colors. "Peachblow," with gradations resembling the nineteenth century art glass by that name, was one of the most popular of these cased lines. Production continued until 1987, when Kanawha was sold to Raymond Dereume Glass Inc. in Punxsutawney, Pennsylvania. This lasted for only two years, closing in 1989.

Of Kanawha's crackle glass production, most people are familiar with the #85 amberina pitcher with the stretched spout. It is also one of few pieces, if not the only one, in modern design. The many Kanawha miniatures, with ruffled rims or applied squiggles look like the countless traditional designs by any one of the companies making crackle miniatures. Larger Kanawha items also copy or interpret designs by other companies. The tall stretched bud vases resemble some Viking or Fenton items. The #148 double-spout water bottle is the Blenko design with a molded motif. The #1163 and #1166 ruffled bowls, and #1168 crimped bowl are also Blenko knock-offs. The #1165 swan bowl is taken from Duncan. Whether borrowing from history or from contemporary factories, Kanawha designs can often be identified by the molded foot and visible seams. Their Hamon production is more challenging, since these hand blown pieces can be mistaken for the work of other companies as well. A piece with a Kanawha label and a pontil scar was probably a Hamon production, because Kanawha normally had a smooth bottom from being molded.

Kanawha colors include: amber, amberina, amethyst, Authentic Cranberry, blue, cranberry, crystal,green, ruby, and yellow.

Pilgrim

One of the few remaining factories responsible for crackle and other handmade glass, the Pilgrim Glass Corporation of Ceredo, West Virginia is headed today by the man who founded it in 1949. Alfred E. Knobler was trained as a ceramic engineer and entered the glass business via pottery sales in the 1930s. During World War II he worked for the War Department as an engineer, but soon returned to pottery and glass sales.

Tri-State Glass of Huntington, West Virginia was headed by Walter Bailey, who at that time was going through a difficult time. Knobler believed that he could turn around the failing company, so in 1949 he purchased it from Bailey. After the addition of a new gas line into the company, Knobler's belief turned into a reality, and success prompted him to expand. After purchasing land in Ceredo (near Huntington) he built the present Pilgrim facility, which opened in 1956. Shortly after, the Corning Museum of Glass featured one of Knobler's designs in its *Glass 1959*.

From the beginning they specialized in free blown crackle glass in vivid colors. The fine "onion" or "Swedish" crackle that Pilgrim is known for, is a result of an additional step in the crackle process. Most crackle is made by simply dipping the hot glass object in cold water, causing it to crack in random patterns over the entire surface. The piece is then reheated to smooth the surface, leaving fine crackle lines as part of the design. Pilgrim, however, rolled the hot blown piece of glass in sawdust before it was reheated and then dipped in the cold water. Like other producers of crackle glass, Pilgrim made large quantities of it in the 1950s and 1960s. Generally, they used colored handles in the 1950s and crystal handles in the 1960s. Some items can be identified as Pilgrim by a mark impressed in the center of the base—either a group of little dots ("strawberry marks") or a group of parallel wavy lines ("water waves"). Like other companies in the area, Pilgrim made a range of decorative objects in both crackled and plain colored glass. They also produced a line of satin finished items; these were given an acid bath to degloss the surface and give a satiny feel to the glass.

Two brothers, Alessandro and Roberto Moretti, came from Italy to work at Pilgrim in the 1950s. Their introduction of glass animals, figurines, and other Venetian style items gave Pilgrim another desirable line. Since Venetian glass imports were becoming popular with American consumers, the Pilgrim Venetian glass met with success. Other Pilgrim innovations included an outstanding shade of pink (cranberry) introduced by plant manager Karel Konrad in 1968. The color was so desirable that it remains a staple today.

For a short time, many Pilgrim items also went under the name Empire, and even a separate catalog was produced. This so-called Empire glass was made at the Pilgrim factory in Ceredo using Pilgrim molds and colors, so without a label they are virtually impossible to distinguish from Pilgrim.

Through the 1970s a line called Kitchen Chemistry included canisters and jars with both utilitarian and aesthetic appeal. Other items introduced about this time were Rock Crystal Pitchers with a bumpy surface, salt and pepper shakers, paperweights, bells, plant hangers, and candle holders. In 1977 and 1978 Pilgrim produced a series of signed studio pieces. These experimental pieces appeared only in their 1977-78 catalog.

The regular designers—Allesandro and Roberto Moretti and their brother-in-law, Mario Sandon, who arrived in 1963, were the creative force at Pilgrim. Born in Italy in 1930 to a family with a glassmaking tradition dating to the seventeenth century, Roberto Moretti apprenticed at Murano glass factories as a boy. Later he attended the Instituto Technico del Vetro. He worked for Fugina delgi Angeli and executed designs by Pablo Picasso, Marc Chagall, and Jean Cocteau. Moretti came to the United States in 1958, and his work attracted national attention at the 1965-66 New York World's Fair. Roberto Moretti was described as "one of the pioneers in this country in a movement for glassworkers to design and form their individual creations." Paul N. Perrot, director of the Corning Museum of Glass wrote in 1968:

> Mr. Moretti's stylized shapes reveal a complete understanding of the fluid properties of glass and the subtle harmonies which can be achieved by understanding its inner light. His work . . . demonstrates that in skillful hands glass is a sculptural medium and that particularly happy results can be achieved when both the originator of the design and its executor are linked in one person.

Moretti retired in 1984 and died in 1986. His older brother Alessandro retired in 1985; Mario Sandon also retired but, on occasion, continued to bring the Murano touch to Pilgrim.

Pilgrim colors include: Amber, Amethyst, Blue, Crystal, Emerald Green, Lemon-Lime, Olive Green, Ruby, Sea Green, Sky Blue, Smoke Crystal, Tangerine, and Topaz.

Rainbow

The Rainbow Art Co. was founded in 1942 in Huntington, West Virginia by Joseph Goudeket and Henry Manus. Originally a glass decorating business, the Rainbow Art Co. turned to producing its own hand blown glass in 1954, and it became the Rainbow Art Glass Co. Like other neighboring companies, they produced blown glass in vivid colors, often with a crackle finish. Rainbow made crackle through the 1970s, which was later than many of its competitors. This may account for the large number of Rainbow crackle items on the market today. In 1973 they were purchased by Viking and continued to make crackle glass until 1979. The Rainbow factory burned down in 1983, and all operations ceased.

Although many of the crackle miniatures, and even larger decanters and bottles, are similar to those made at these other companies, Rainbow made a number of distinctive forms. These can often be identified by large round or elongated teardrop-shaped stoppers. The top of the bottle neck normally has a flat collar, which also helps to differentiate Rainbow pieces. Paper labels, which identify the company may also aid in dating. In the case of Rainbow, the gold and black sun ray label is the earliest. The later silver bubble with black lettering was used on items that were sold wholesale. The same label with red lettering was used on those sold in the retail store, because they were considered "seconds."

The company mainstay was the crackle and plain miniature vases and pitchers that are so common in the marketplace today. Among the other more common items are copies and interpretations: Rainbow #9025 and #9055 decanter is almost identical to the Blenko model; the #512 optic pitcher resembles Anderson's early Blenko pitcher, but the Rainbow version has a narrowed neck and an added foot. Rainbow's contribution to mid-century design was neither these knock-offs nor the proliferation of ruffled miniatures. It was the occasional inspired design that Rainbow will be remembered for—like the decanter with ivy vase stopper, the tall slender bottle with long stopper, the pitcher with three-ring handle, or the decanters with oversized ball or flame stopper.

Rainbow colors include: Amber, Amberina, Amethyst, Blue, Crystal, Golden Amber, New Turquoise, Olive Green, Orange/Amberina, Pink, Ruby, Smoke, and Tangerina.

Viking

The Viking Glass Company was originally called the New Martinsville Glass Manufacturing Company, which was incorporated in 1900. Like many other glass companies, New Martinsville began by making utilitarian glass and soon expanded into more ornamental items. Among their first of these were lines of colorful opalescent art glass and decorative pressed wares. Throughout the 1920s, new products were continually offered in distinctive colors.

Financial problems plagued the glass industry as much as any other in the 1930s, and the company went into receivership in 1937. A group from Connecticut purchased it and reopened as the New Martinsville Glass Co. Then, in 1944, former partner G.R. Cummings purchased all of the New Martinsville stock and changed the name to Viking Glass Company because of its reference to Scandinavia and its modern glass designs.

New Martinsville Glass can be divided into three periods : 1) 1901-07, Art and opaque glass such as Peachblow; 2) 1907-37, Pattern glass with a heavy deep pattern and brilliancy; 3) 1937-44, Crystal and some colored wares and novelty and decorative items such as candlesticks and figurines. Under the new Viking name and ownership, color became a focus. Their subsidiary, Rainbow Art Glass of Huntington (established 1939), also relied heavily of color for its identity and appeal. Both Rainbow and Viking were featured in the Corning Museum's *Glass 1959.* One of Viking's most distinctive and popular lines, called Epic, began in the early 1960s. Epic included unusual shapes that seemed to play on the drippy quality of hot glass. Long, slender-tailed birds, sometimes mounted on container lids, became other Viking trademarks. Elmer E. Miller, who joined the company in 1923, was responsible for many of the modern designs of the 1950s and 1960s.

Viking was one of the leading West Virginia companies to contribute to American mid-century glass, but it was different from others like Blenko or Pilgrim. Rather than off-hand glass, Viking focused on fine-quality molded wares, and the forms were rarely copied by other factories. Except for a few designs closely shared with Fenton, most of Viking's plain-finish glass is exclusive to Viking and therefore very easy to identify. Among the only important crackle that Viking made were their patio lights and large heavy ashtrays. The remainder of its limited crackle production consists mostly of plain bud vases, which can easily be mistaken for the work of other companies.

Kenneth Dalzell, the fourth generation of an eighty-four year family presidency of the Fostoria Glass Company, joined Lancaster Colony when it purchased Fostoria in 1983. Then, when Fostoria closed, Dalzell left Lancaster to head his own glass company again. He reopened Viking as Dalzell-Viking in 1987. The company continued to make high quality hand-molded glass in both crystal and vibrant colors such as ruby red and cobalt blue. In addition to decorative giftware sold at department stores and specialty shops, Dalzell-Viking made reproductions of early glass for clients such as the Smithsonian, the Metropolitan Museum of Art, Oneida, Coca-Cola, and the Heisey Collector Club. Like neighboring Blenko, Pilgrim, and Fenton, Viking was a survivor in a shrinking American handmade glass industry until it closed in 1998.

Viking colors include: amber, amberina, amethyst, blue, brown, crystal, green, ruby, and tangerine.

Chapter One: Stoppers

Decanters

Blenko #445 decanter in Honey, with rosettes on stopper and around base. 12" h. $100-150

Rainbow #9848 Tangerina decanter with extravagant twisted flame stopper. 14" h. $150-200

Opposite page:
Blenko #920 Sea Green, Jonquil, Olive Green, and Tangerine decanters in small, medium, and large sizes, designed by Winslow Anderson c. 1950. 10-1/2", 16-1/2", and 22" h. $40-60, $60-80, $100-125

Left: Blenko #948 award-winning decanter in Jonquil (with handled placed high), designed by Winslow Anderson c. 1950. Right: Pilgrim #24 "Modern" copy (with low handle) in Tangerine, both 13" h. $125-175; $70-90

Blenko designs by Wayne Husted:
#6123S Rosé bottle-decanter in rare and desirable color. 11" h. $75-100
#6123M Jonquil bottle-decanter. 13-1/2" h. $75-100
626M Tangerine bulbous bottle-decanter. 18" h. $125-175

Opposite page:
Blenko decanters by Wayne Husted:
#5826M Sea Green. 20-1/2" h. $100-150
#6029 Tangerine decanter with oversized stopper. 27-1/2" h. $150-250
#628S Olive Green decanter with very slender body. 24-5/8" h. $100-150

Left to right:
Blenko designed by Joel Myers:
#7411 Honey. 13-1/2" h. $70-90
#7126 Crystal. 14" h. $60-80
#6626S Olive Green. 15" h. $75-100

Blenko:
#6629 Olive Green by Joel Myers. 12-5/8" h. $75-100
#5815S Sea Green by Wayne Husted. 17" h. $80-100
#6516 Turquoise (Blenko Blue) by Joel Myers. 14-1/2" h. $75-100

Blenko:
#6630S Olive Green by Myers. 9" h. $50-60
#37 Blenko Blue designed in 1937 and produced for decades. 13" h. $50-60
#708 Ruby by Myers, similar to the candle-vase. 7-1/2' h. $40-50

Opposite page:
Blenko "figural" shaped decanters:
#7036 Olive Green decanter by Joel Myers. 17" h. $125-175
#5521 Amethyst decanter by Wayne Husted. 11" h. $125-175

Blenko Tangerine (amberina):
- #6212S footed with flame stopper, by Husted. 16" h. $90-110
- #649 bubble shaped by Myers. 13" h. $80-100
- #6944 with molded stopper by Myers. 9-1/2" h. $60-70
- #49 pinched by Winslow Anderson. 10-1/2" h. $50-60

eft to right:
lenko:
#719 Blenko Blue, by Myers. 17" h. $60-80
#6027 Blenko Blue pencil-neck with shot-glass stopper by Husted. 17" h. $125-150

lenko 12" 627S in lenko Blue and 8" #627L in live Green, by usted. $50-60; 75-100

lenko 22" 6311L in angerine and 5" #6311M in osé, by usted. $125-75; $75-100

lenko 16-1/2" 6122S in angerine and 1-1/2" #6122L Sea Green, by usted. $75-00; $100-125

Left: Rainbow 15" #9060 Tangerina decanter with large teardrop or flame stopper
Right: 14" New Turquoise. $125-150; $100-125

Rainbow #9024 in Amethyst and Ruby, with Rainbow #9768 Ruby (top right). 11-14" h. $75-125 each

Opposite page, top to bottom:
Bischoff 8" decanters with Crystal stoppers: #372 Amethyst and Gold, and #556 Mint Green. $50-60 each

Kanawha:
- #710R ringed decanters in blue and green, with #710 amberina. 9" h. $35-45 each
- #715 amberina and amber. 13" h. $50-60 each

HAND CRAFTED
Bischoff

Bischoff:
#373 Lime with Crystal handle and stopper. 17-1/2" h. $60-80
#152 Charcoal with Crystal handle and stopper. 17" h. $60-80
#478 Mint Green pinched with Crystal stopper. 11" h. $40-50

Rainbow. Left: 14" #9708 Amberina with rings; right: 24" #9001 Smoke with rings. $70-90; $125-175

Rainbow. Left: #799 "The Admiral" 14" New Turquoise. Right: #9610 16" Blue. $60-80 each

Rainbow 13" #1660 Ruby and Amethyst, with variant in Amberina. $60-80 each

Rainbow, left to right: #16126 Amberina 12"; #9621 Tangerina 11"; #6021 Ruby 11" decanter. $50-60 each

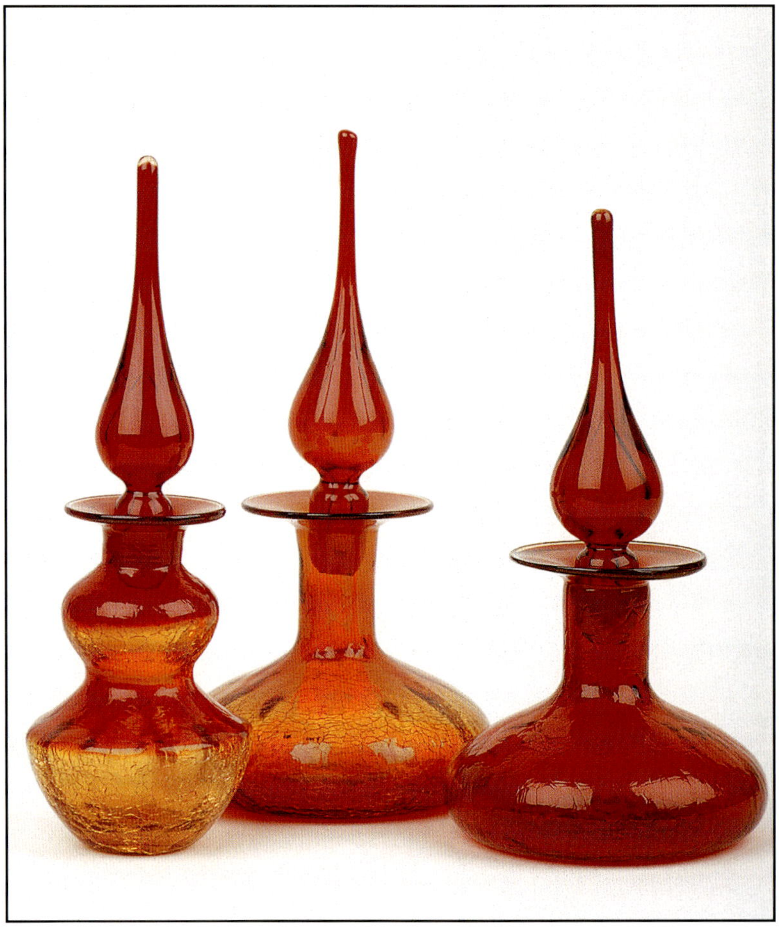

Left: Rainbow #9613S Golden Amber 14" decanter. Center and right: Kanawha #714 blue and green 13" decanters. $50-60 each

Opposite page, top to bottom:
Left to right:
Kanawha #720 ruby pinched. 14" h. $50-60
Kanawha # 716 green. 10-1/2" h. $40-50
Possibly Hamon, butterscotch. 10" h. $40-50

Rainbow #811 decanters: Emerald Green, Amethyst, Tangerina, New Turquoise (earlier). 11" average h. $30-40 each

Pilgrim with teardrop stoppers:

#22 "Classic" in Lemon-Lime. 15" h. $50-60
#23R "Pilgrim" in Ruby. 19" h. $50-60
#21 "Orleans" in Sky Blue. 19" h. $50-60
#20 "Scandia" in Olive Green. 15" h. $40-50

Rainbow:
#9705 Tangerina. 12-1/2" h. $60-80
#9705 earlier model in Amethyst. 13" h. $70-90
#863 Golden Amber. 16-1/2" h. $70-90
#933 Ruby. 13-1/2" h. $60-80

Pilgrim:
#19 "Gurgle" in Tangerine. 22" h. $150-200
#18 "Newport" in Amethyst. 19" h. $80-130
#12 "Dew Drop" in Tangerine. 22" h. $125-175

Rainbow bubble stoppers, no collar:

- #9823 Golden Amber and Orange/ Amberina. 10-1/2" h. $60-80 each
- #9821 Golden Amber. 16-1/2" h. $100-150
- #9822 Orange/ Amberina. 12-1/2" h. $70-90

Rainbow bubble stopper, with collar:
- #16101 Amberina. 14" h. $80-120
- #16103 Amberina. 6" h. $40-50
- #16102 Orange/ Amberina. 12" h. $70-90

Left to right:
Blenko #638M Husted design in Jonquil with bubble stopper. 15" h. $75-100

Rainbow #9010 Pink with collar and bubble stopper. 11" h. $70-90

Rainbow #935 Ruby with large bubble stopper. 11" h. $75-100

Opposite page:
Rainbow with bubble stopper and collar:
#9010 Ruby. 11" h. $70-90
#9011 Pink. 13-1/2" h. $80-100
#810 Blue. 8" h. $50-60

Rainbow with bubble stopper and collar:
#9757 Amberina 8" h. $60-70
#9625 Amberina 9" h. $60-80
#9055 Amethyst 10-1/2" h. $70-90
#1672 New Turquoise 7" h. $50-60

Rainbow bubble stopper:
Orange/ Amberina 8" h. $40-60
#9757 Orange/ Amberina 7" h. $35-45
#16102 Orange/ Amberina 10" h. $70-90
#6212 Ruby 9" h. $60-80

Rainbow triple-ball:
#343 Tangerina 9" h. $50-70
#9761 Real Ruby 10" h. $60-80
#9760 Golden Amber 12-1/2" h. $75-100
#343 Amethyst 9" h. $50-70

Small decanters attributed to Rainbow. $30-40 each

Top to bottom:
Blenko Crystal with Honey trim, by Joel Myers:
#6838-CH with applied rings. 16" h. $100-125
#6821 with stars. 14" h. $75-100

Detail

Blenko Crystal with Turquoise trim:
#49 pinched 10-1/2" h. $50-60
#475 with rings and heavy stopper. 14" h. $100-150

Rainbow Bathroom Boutique Collection. $45-65 each:
#C334 Crystal with Golden Amber 8" h.
#C340 Crystal with Golden Amber 11-1/2" h.
#C330 Crystal with Golden Amber 8-1/2" h.
#C333 Crystal with Green 8" h.

Blue Del (of Huntington) pinched crystal with crystal trim. 10" and 13" h. $50-70 each

CRUETS

Rainbow #891 cruets with double ball stopper in various colors. 6" h. $25-35 each

Rainbow #891 cruets of another shape, with double ball stopper in various colors. $25-35 each

Rainbow 6" #1611 and 7" #1606 Amberina cruets with double ball stopper. $25-35 each

Group of cruets in various colors attributed to Pilgrim and Hamon. 5-1/2" average h. $20-25 each

Left: Rainbow #891 cruets wit double ball stopper in Olive Green, Crystal, and Amberina. $25-35 each

Right: Amethys and turquoise cruets attribute to Hamon. 7" h $20-25 each

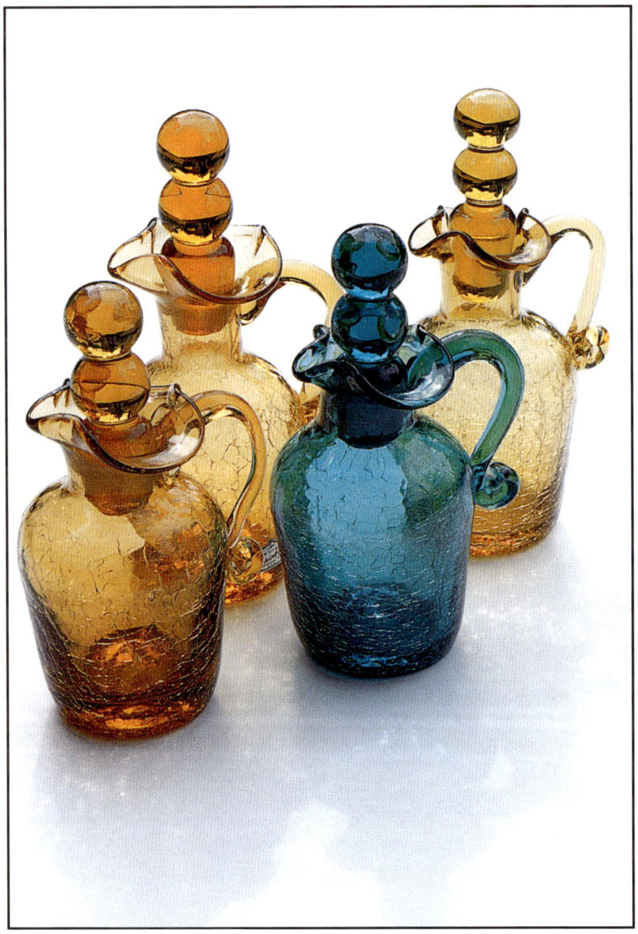

Left: Rainbow #891 cruets in Golden Amber and New Turquoise. 6-1 h. $20-25 each

Right: Two blu cruets and a perfume bottle by Blue Del. $20-25 each

Left to right:
Rainbow Cranberry Flash cruet, early. 6-1/2" h. $40-50

Rainbow #891 Ruby and #9958 Blue cruets. $20-25 each

Pilgrim C110 cruets in Emerald Green and Tangerine. 6-1/2" h. $20-25 each

Rainbow cruets:
#798 Green 8" h. $30-50
#9797M "Bristol Bottle" in Ruby. 8" h. $30-50
Emerald Green 6" h. $20-25
#9056 "Bristol Bottle" in Ruby with Amber handle. 6" h. $20-25

Rainbow 9707 Amberina, Blue, and Tangerina decanters in cruet shape. 8-11" h. $40-60 each

Rainbow Bathroom Boutique Collection:
C326 Crystal with Blue 8-1/2" h. $50-60
C333 Crystal with Green 8" h. $50-60

Kanawha #21 blue and amberina cruets with metal lids. 7" h. 15-20 each

Rainbow:
#6811 Orange/Amberina. 7-12" h. $20-25
#D402 Golden Amber with Ruby. 7" h. $20-25
#9951 Golden Amber. 10" h. $30-35

Group of early cruets attributed to Rainbow. 7" h. $20-25 each

Gibson c. 1999 vaseline and cobalt cruets. 7-1/2" and 3-1/2" h. $20-30 each

Bischoff. $20-25 each:
- #600 Peacock Blue. 5-1/4" h.
- #422 Peacock Blue and Emerald Green. 6-1/2" h.
- #601 Amethyst and Emerald Green. 6" h.

HAND BLOWN BY
Rainbow

Rainbow:
#9028 in New Turquoise and Amethyst. 9" h. $35-45 each
#9028S in Olive Green and Blue. 6-1/2" h. $20-25 each

Opposite page, top to bottom:
Rainbow 6" #9056 "Bristol Bottles" in Golden Amber and Ruby with similar style in Emerald Green. $20-25 each

Rainbow cruets. $20-25 each
#403 Olive Green and Ruby. 6-1/2" h.
#401 Blue and Orange-Amberina. 7" h.
##402 Olive Green. 7" h.

Bischoff #237 cruets in Lime and Peacock Blue. 9" h. $35-45 each

Rainbow #9028S Blue and Olive Green. 6-1/2" h. $20-25 each

Pilgrim #C112 Olive Green with dropover handle and Topaz. 6-1/2" h. $20-25 each

Pilgrim #C110 Ruby with ribbed handle and Blue. 6" h. $20-25

Pilgrim C113 Tangerine. 6" h. $20-25 each

Yellow cruets attributed to Kanawha. 5" average height. $15-20 each

Blenko #948S bent cruet in Jonquil, by Winslow Anderson. 8-5/8" h. $50-70 each

Pilgrim C111 Blue. 10-1/2" h. $25-35 each

Chapter 2: Vases

Pilgrim vases with applied rope:
- #673 Amber 7" h. $35-45
- #73 Smoke 12" h. $60-70
- #473 Ruby 5" h. $15-20
- #92 Amber and Blue 15" h. $80-100
- #773 Emerald Green 7" h. $20-30

Group of cylindrical vases with ruffled tops in Ruby, Amberina, and Blue, attributed to Rainbow. 6-10" h. $20-70 each

Group of vases with ruffled tops attributed to Bischoff. 5-10" h. $20-80 each

Early Flashed Cranberry vases made by Rainbow after Blenko designs. 9" h. $60-80 each

Kanawha #38 ruby and yellow swing vases. 17" h. $40-50 each

Blenko:
Tangerine bottle vase. 11" h. $35-45
#6323L Tangerine. 12-1/2" h. $55-65
#7223 Tangerine swing. 24" h. $100-125
#7012S Blenko Blue. 7" h. $25-30

Rainbow Ruby:
Bottom: #881 miniature 4" h. $10-15
Left: Pinched waist with ruffled tops. 5-1/2" and 6" h. $20-25 each
Right: #6115 cylindrical with ruffled top. 6" h. $25-30
Top: #R530 swing vase. 13" h. $30-40
#97545 flared top. 5-1/2" h. $23-30

Blenko:
#413L Tangerine giant goblet. 13" h. $50-60
#6524S Tangerine footed vase. 13" h. $55-65
Olive green vases attributed to Blenko .8-1/2" and 9-1/4" h. $30-40 each

Blenko Olive Green:
#439L fan top. 13" h. $60-80
#6422 pencil neck with collar. 16-3/4" h. $100-125
#6614 squat vase. 5" h. $25-35
#439S fan top. 7-1/2" h. $25-35

Blenko later:
#Antique Green bottle vase. 10" h. $25-35
#872 fan vase in Amethyst. 11-1/2" h. $40-50
#8813M bag vase in Orchid. 9-1/2" h. $25-35

Pilgrim Blue Fan Vase. 12" h. $70-90

Pilgrim 12" #66 bulbous vase in Ruby; with Pilgrim 5" #475 in Blue. $60-70; $10-15

Opposite page, top to bottom:
Variety of Kanawha vases with ruffled tops. 5"-10" h. $15-25 each

Blenko Turquoise (Blenko Blue):
#63A2 bottle by Husted. 9-1/2" h. $20-25
#7419 bottle by Nickerson. 11" h. $30-40
#6010 with folded top, by Husted. 10-3/4" h. $100-125
#390 crimped top vase. 8" h. $45-55

Viking with pinched waist:
#7550 blue (copy of Blenko #533) 9-1/2" h. $20-25
#7458 green. 9" h. $20-25
#7557 blue ball vase. 10-1/2" h. $50-60
#7553 tangerine. 7" h. $20-25
#7554 blue pitcher. 7" h. $20-25

Blenko:
#3620L Amethyst 9" vase. $40-50
#428S Olive Green 9" footed vase. $40-50

Group of Bischoff and Pilgrim indented vases (after Winslow Anderson's Blenko design c. 1950). 5-1/2" to 11" h. $20-30 small $50-60 large

Pilgrim vases:
#507 Amethyst. 5-1/2" h. $30-40
#60 Topaz. 9" h. $30-40
#64 "Flip" Vase in Ruby. 12" h. $40-50
#750 Sky Blue. 5-1/2" h. $20-30

Rainbow flashed cranberry 9" footed vase. $60-80

Bischoff #568 Charcoal with Crystal trim (copy of Blenko #473 from 1947). 7" h. $30-40

Opposite page:
Blenko #388 crimped vases in Amethyst, Olive Green, and Wheat. $40-50 each

Kanawha #1145 ruby with applied rigaree and ruffled top. 5" h. $15-20
Kanawha 10" amberina. $40-50
Kanawha ruby with rigaree. 6-7" h. $20-30 each

Ruffled vases attributed to Kanawha. 4-1/2" to 6" h. $10-20 each

Group of Rainbow vases with ruffled top, two with rigaree. $15-20 each

Left: Bischoff Peacock Blue with crimped tops. $20-30 each:
- #471 fan vase (top). 6-1/2" h.
- #416 footed vase (left). 7-1/2" h.
- #507B bowl. 5" d.
- #974 footed vase. 6-1/2" h.

Right: Bischoff Peacock Blue footed vases. $25-35 each:
- #244 (left) 8" h.
- #518 ruffled top (back). 11" h.
- #466 (right) 11 h.

Left: Blenko #6843-TO Turquoise with Olive trim. 8-1/2" h. $60-70

Right: Bischoff Peacock Blue:
- 3-1/2" miniature (left). $10-12
- #411 dented vase (back). 6-1/2" h. $20-30
- #507H hat vase (right). 6" h. $20-30

Blenko Honey hibiscus vases. $25-35 each

Pilgrim Ruby #61 square top 12" and #815 square top 10" vases. $40-60 each

Blenko pinched waist:
#5519L Sea Green 16" h. $50-60
#5318 pale Amethyst. 7-1/2" h. $20-25
#5519M Ruby 11 h. $30-40

Right: Blenko #9909 Azure 14" footed vase from 1999 (with #5519L). $40-50

Left: Blenko #442L Wild Rose Crystal Beaker Vase with Amethyst rosettes. 13-1/2" h. $125-175

Right: Blenko #423S Wild Rose Crystal Urn with Sky Blue rosettes. 8" h. $60-80

Left: Left: Blenko #336ML Leaf Vase in Crystal with Sea Green leaves. 10" h. $90-110
Right: Blenko #33L Leaf Bowl in Crystal with Turquoise leaves. 4-1/2" h. $50-60

Right: Blenko 1998 designs by Matt Carter:
- #9815L Crystal with Cobalt foot. 10-1/2" h. $35-45
- #9816S Crystal with Kiwi foot. 10-1/4" h. $35-45

Left: Blenko #473 Ear vase in Crystal with Teal ears. 8" h. $75-100
Right: Blenko #5195 Oval vase in Crystal with Turquoise trim. 7" h. $75-100

Blenko Crystal Bell Vases:
- #428S with Teal foot. 7" h. $40-60
- #58L with Emerald Green foot. 9" h. $50-70
- #58 with Amethyst foot. 7" h. $40-60

Blenko #487 Crimp vase in Crystal with Emerald trim. 8" h. $75-100

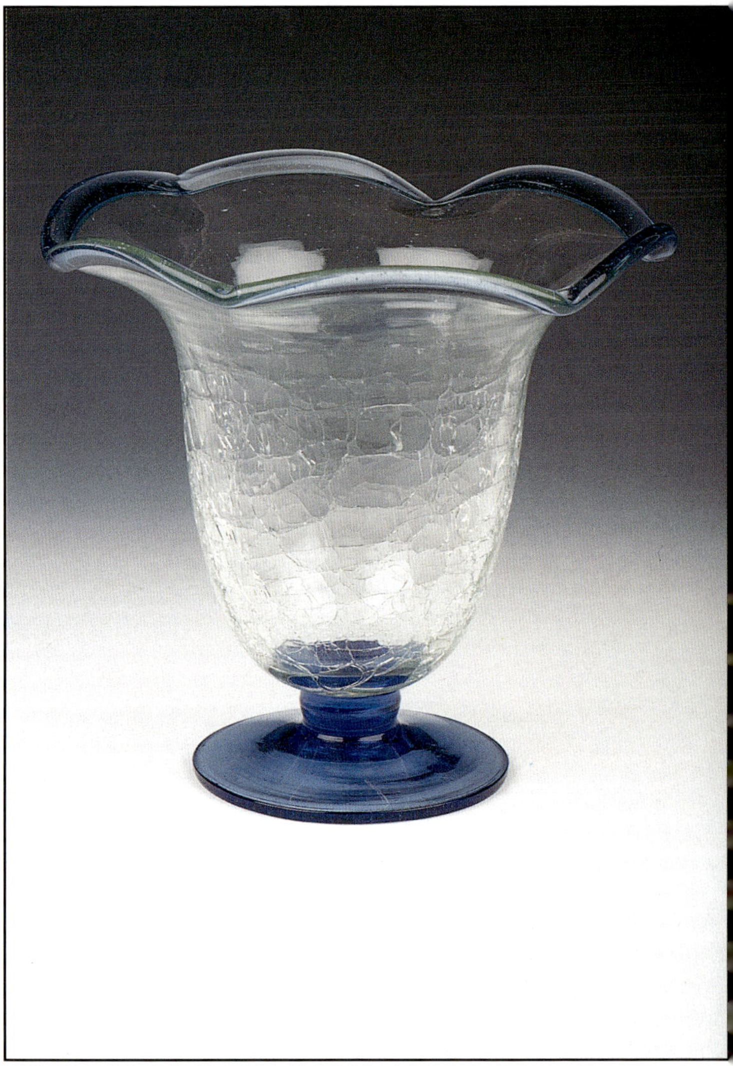

Blenko (attributed) Crystal with Turquoise trim and foot. 7" h. $50-60

Opposite page, top to bottom:
Blenko #482 in three sizes: 7" small; 9-1/2" medium; and 11" large. $40-50, $50-60, $60-80

Blenko Crystal:
#7141. 9" h. $35-45
#9432 with Cobalt trim. 8-1/2" h. $40-60
#8318 with Kiwi trim. 6-3/4" h. $40-60
#7419. 11" h. $40-50

Top: Bischoff Charcoal #A-3B vase with two Charcoal handles. 5-1/2" h. $30-40
Left & right: Similar 8-1/2" vases, amethyst possibly Bischoff and Blenko #490S Sea Green urn. $30-40 each

Below, left to right: Blenko #488L 12" Sea Green Vase with Crystal handles. $50-60

Bischoff vases with crystal handles:
- #514 Amethyst 8" h. $30-40
- #258 Charcoal. 9-1/2" h. $40-50
- #483 Emerald Green 15" h. $60-80

Chapter 3: Handles

Kanawha green pitchers:
#277 pulled lip. 7-3/4" h. $20-25
#149 gourd. 7-1/2" h. $20-25
#226 flat base. 7-1/4" h. $15-20
#6-8H with shoulder. 7" h. $15-20
#280 bulbous base. 6-1/2" h. $15-20
#232 folded top. 5" h. $10-15
#14 with sticker. 5" h. $10-15

Kanawha #85, common in amberina, but rarely seen in various other colors. $50-60 each (amberina $30-40)

Rainbow pitchers:
#9946 Blue. 10-1/2" h. $35-45
#9945 Golden Amber. 7-1/2" h. $25-30
#9802 Emerald Green. 10-1/2" h. $40-50

Pilgrim #56 Lemon Lime 15" pitcher and Topaz 13" variant. $40-50 each

Rainbow:
#9758 Golden Amber Gurgle. 9" h. $40-60
#97595 Amethyst Gurgle. 5-1/2" h. $20-30
#A-6009 Amethyst. 9" h. $40-50

Bischoff #8661G Gold 18-1/2" jug, shown with Bischoff M-11 in Peacock Blue to show relative size. $75-100; $10-15

Pilgrim #62 Emerald Green 12" jug, with Pilgrim 755 Amethyst miniature. $50-60; $15-20

Opposite page:
Bischoff cylindrical pitchers with crystal handles:
- #330 Green. 13-1/2" h. $70-90
- #240M Emerald Green. 9-1/2" h. $40-60
- #103 Peacock Blue. 9-1/2" h. $40-60

Bischoff Poinsettia Red small and medium pitchers; with 14-1/2" #719, all with Crystal handles. $15-20; $25-35; $50-70

Blenko Tangerine #6030 pitchers in 10-1/2", 13", and 18-1/2" h. $40-50, $60-70, and $100-125

Left: Bischoff #308 Gold Martini Pitcher (without stirrer). 8-3/4" h. $25-35

Right: Pilgrim #55 pitchers (copies of Blenko design) in Ruby and Tangerine with Crystal handles. 15" h. $40-50 each

Left: Blenko #546 by Wayne Husted. 11" h. $50-60

Right: Pilgrim #51 pitcher with Morgantown style slant top in Sea Green and Tangerine. 11-1/2" h. $40-50 each

Bischoff Peacock Blue:
#M-11 miniature. $10-15
#257M bulbous. 6-1/2" h. $15-20
#311-2 bulbous. 9" h. $30-40
#214 long neck. 15" h. $50-60
#234 (top left) handled vase. 10" h. $30-40

Left: Blenko #544 Husted 1954 design in Tangerine. 8-3/4" h. $50-70
Center: Bischoff #324 Gold. 10-1/2" h. $30-40
Right: Bischoff #926 Orange with thin neck. 11" h. $30-40

Bischoff with Crystal handles:
#8121 Emerald Green. 9-1/2" h. $35-45
Green, attributed to Bischoff. 7" h. $20-25
#441 Lime. 7-1/2" h. $20-30
#331-1/2 Peacock. 5-1/2" h. $15-20

Pilgrim #57 pitcher in Amber and in Smoke, with #47 in Blue with Crystal handle. 9-1/2" h. $30-40 each

Pilgrim pitchers:
#28 Sea Green. 8-1/2" h. $25-35
Lemon-Lime 9" h. $25-35
#49 Sea Green. 13" h. $35-45

Blenko #6414 Olive Green 9-1/2" pitcher (left) with unidentified olive green and amberina pitchers. $40-50; $25-35

Blenko #6714 in Tangerine and Wheat. 9" h. $35-45

Bischoff Amethyst and gray pitchers with Crystal handles, and Bischoff #947 Gold 8" with flamboyant handle. $25-35 each; $40-50

Bischoff pitchers. $25-35 each:
#187 Green (top). 8" h.
#213 Green. 7-3/4" h.
#8125 Lime. 8-1/4" h.

Blenko #668L in Honey with #668S in Olive Green. 7-1/4" and 6-1/4" h. $25-45 each

Kanawha with molded grape motif:
#289 green pitcher. 9" h. $35-45
#288 yellow pitcher. 11" h. $45-55
#246 blue decanter. 15-1/2" h. $70-90

Blenko #656M and #656S Turquoise pitchers. 10-1/2" and 8-1/2" h. $50-60 and $30-40

Blenko pitchers:
#361P Charcoal. 7" h. $35-45
#6512 Wheat. 6" h. $25-35
#939P Amethyst. 14-1/2" h. $60-70

Rainbow pitchers:
#9709 Newport in Tangerina. 8-1/2" h. $30-40
#9864 Olive Green. 7-1/2" h. $25-35
#6125 Pink. 8" h. $30-40

Pilgrim #52 pitchers in Blue and Amber (copy of Blenko #939P). 13" h. $35-45

Blenko #637L in Tangerine (center) with #637M in Turquoise and Ruby/Tangerine pitchers. 8-1/2" and 7-1/2" h. $30-45 each

Ruby and smoke pitchers attributed to Hamon. 7-1/2" h. $20-30

Left: 11" amberina pitcher. $30-40
Center & right: Unidentified 8" orange and blue pitchers. $15-25 each

Rainbow jugs with cork stoppers. $20-30 each:
#236 Crystal 7" h.
#328 Olive Green 11" h.
#327 Tangerina and Amethyst 8" h.
#7256 Dark Topaz (Viking) 8" h.

Unidentified 11-1/2" and 10" amber pitchers and 11" blue jug. $20-30 each

One amber and several blue pitchers by Blenko. 5" to 7-1/2" h. $20-25 each

Group of amberina pitchers attributed to Kanawha. 8"-9" h. $15-25 each

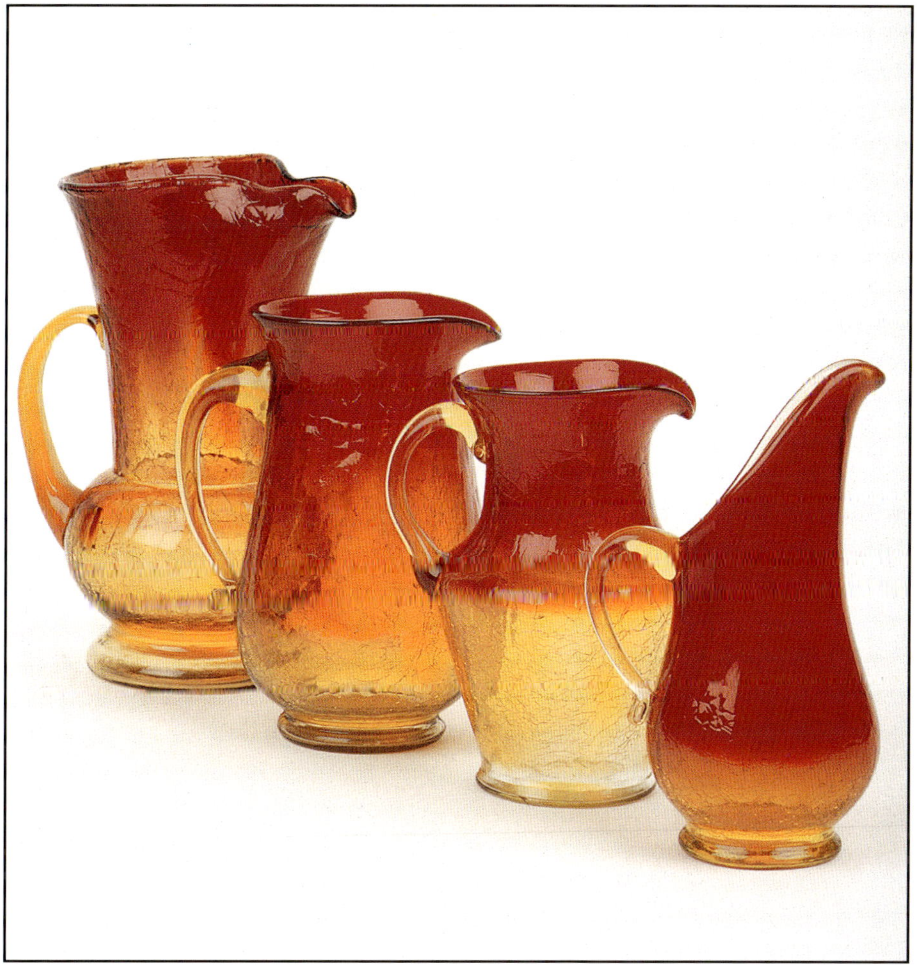

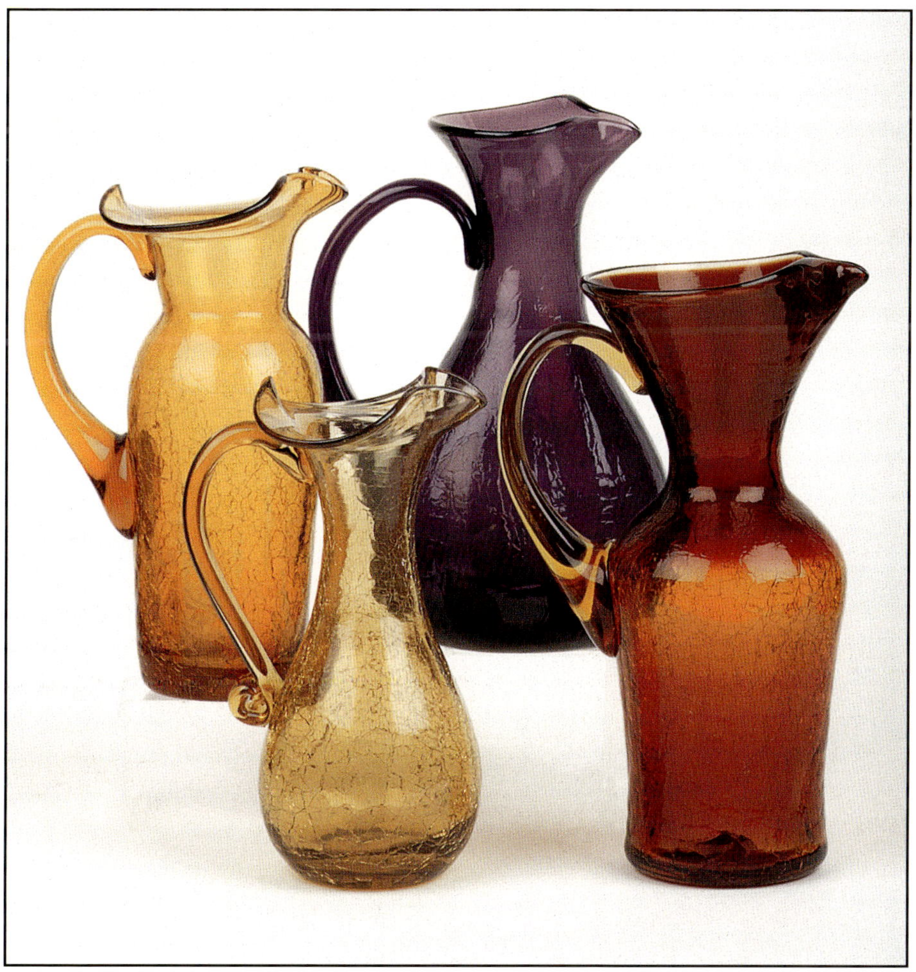

Rainbow pitchers $20-35 each:
- #9704 Golden Amber. 8-1/2" h.
- #637 Amber. 6-1/2" h.
- #6154 Amethyst. 9" h.
- #16121 Amberina. 9-1/2"

Rainbow pitchers: $15-25 each
#6134 Ruby (top). 7-1/2" h.
#62 Ruby (center left). 5-1/2" h.
#1612 Amberina (center right). 5-1/2" h.
Tangerina 4-1/2", Blue, and Amberina (front)

Group of amberina pitchers attributed to Kanawha. 6-1/2" to 9" h. $20-35 each

Blenko #667L Turquoise and #667S Tangerine. 6" and 4-1/4" h. $25-40 each

Rainbow pitchers. $20-35 each:
#9671 New Turquoise and Amethyst (top). 7-1/2" h.
#9774 Blue and Tangerina. 7-1/2" h.
#9671 Blue. 7-1/2" h.
#9773 Golden Amber. 8-1/2" h.

Kanawha "Authentic Cranberry" pitchers. $25-30 each
#6-8-C 8" vase, similar to pitcher.
#6-8H-C 8" pitcher.
#232-C 5" h.
#242-C 4" h.
#264-C 4-1/4" h.
#252-C 4" h.

Rainbow #16099 Amberina and #9769 Amethyst 7" pitchers. $20-30 each

Rainbow pitchers. $15-25 each:
#731 Pink, two New Turquoise, and Blue (right). 6" h.
#9711 New Turquoise. 7-1/2" h.
#16099 Green. 7" h.

Rainbow pitchers. $15-25 each
#9061 New Turquoise (top left). 7-1/2" h.
#154 Ruby (top right). 5" h.
#16124 Amberina. 6" h.
#16125 Amberina. 5" h.
#6112 Amberina. 7" h.

Blenko pitchers. $40-50 each:
#546 Turquoise. 10-3/4" h.
Turquoise 11" h. (attributed)
#6619 Amberina 11" h.

Blenko #623L Turquoise. 10" h.
$40-50
Amber 10" and Amethyst 8-1/2"
attributed to Blenko. $35-45

Kanawha pitchers:
Light amber 7" attributed to
Kanawha. $15-20
#88 blue 9" h. $20-30
#87 yellow 11" h. $35-45

Blenko pitchers $25-40 each:
#938 Antique Green. 10" h.
Turquoise attributed to Blenko. 10" h.
#623S Olive Green. 8" h.

Rainbow pitchers:
#9624 Hancock in Ruby (top). 6" h. $15-20
#16106 Amberina. 7" h. $20-25
#16107 Amberina. 4-1/2" h. $10-15

Group of ruby pitchers attributed to Kanawha. 5" to 7" h. $10-20 each

Pilgrim Group B pitchers. 5-1/2"-6" h. $10-20 each: #516 Emerald Green; #500 Ruby; #504 Lemon-Lime; #502 Tangerine; #506 Amber; #413 Ruby.

Pilgrim Group B pitchers. 5-1/2"-6-1/4" h. $10-20 each #508 Topaz; #503 Ruby; #512 Lemon-Lime; #501 Blue (vase); #517 Tangerine; and Amethyst.

Pilgrim Group B pitchers.5-1/2" to 6-1/4" h. $10-20 each #517 Topaz; #516 Ruby; #506 Olive Green; Blue and Ruby unidentified numbers.

Pilgrim Group C pitchers. Average 7" h. $15-25 each
#684 Ruby; #676 Sea Green; Blue; #675 Topaz; #672 Smoke.

Pilgrim Group C pitchers. Average 7" h. $15-25 each
#682 Ruby; #677 Emerald Green; #685 Topaz; 683 Olive Green

Pilgrim Group C pitchers. Average 7" h. $15-25 each
#673 Amber; #680 Ruby; #672 Emerald Green and Topaz; #683 Tangerine.

Group of medium pitchers attributed to Hamon. 6"-7" h. $15-20 each

Kanawha miniatures. $10-15 each
#159 blue hat; #160 amberina cup; #158 amberina mug; #177 green cups.

Three light green sugar and cream sets attributed to Jamestown in Virginia. 3-1/2", 4", and 6" h. $25-35 set

Kanawha crystal pitchers with blue handles. Average 6" h. $15-20 each
#242 (two); #280 (two); #284; #14.

Opposite page, top left to top right:
Blenko #442P Crystal with Turquoise reeded handle. 7-1/2" h. $35-45

Blenko Crystal jugs:
#443 with Emerald handle. 16" h. $100-125
#417 with Turquoise handle. 7" h. $25-35

Blenko Crystal pitchers:
#361P with Emerald handle. 7" h. $35-45
#3750L with Turquoise handle. $30-40

Chapter 4: Beverage Sets & Tableware

Blenko #49 Turquoise 10-1/2" decanter with #36 Turquoise whiskey glasses. $50-60; $12-18 each

Pilgrim #10 Sky Blue 3-pint, 6-1/2" pitcher and #613-J 5-oz.tumblers (copy of Blenko). $25-35; $10-20 each

Kanawha blue 9" #88 pitcher and #225 tumblers. $25-35; $10-15 each

Gibson iridescent carnival sprayed blue pitcher and glasses, c. 1977. $50-60; $15-25 each

Opposite page:
Green decanter, inspired by Blenko designs, with whiskey glasses. $50-60; $8-12 each

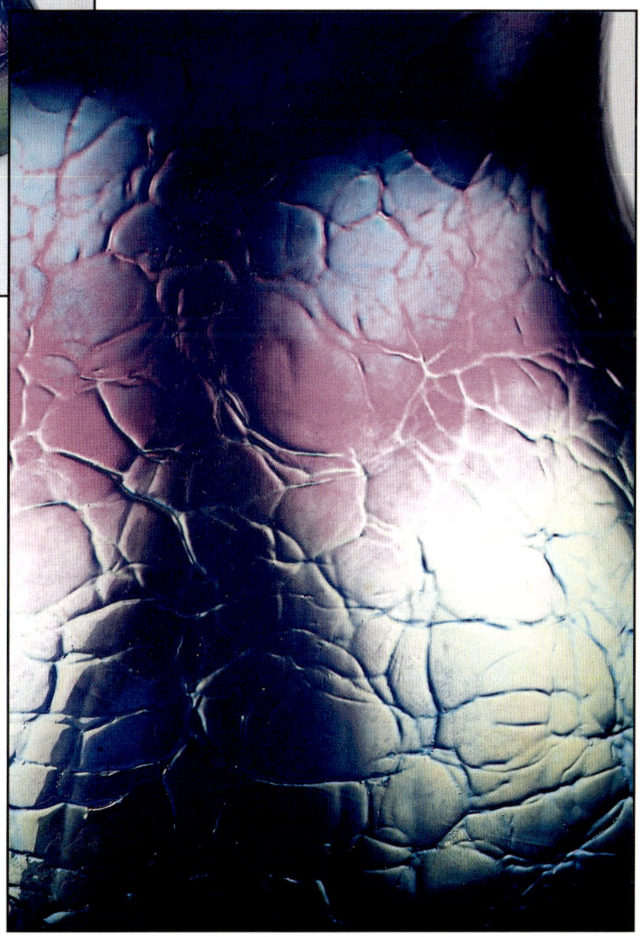

Detail.

Green pitcher with crystal handle with Pilgrim #613J 5-oz. Sea Green tumblers. $25-35; $10-20 each

Amethyst pitcher with Pilgrim #613HB 14-oz. Amethyst tumblers $25-35; $10-20 each

Pilgrim #53, 3-qt. Smoke "Party" Pitcher and #613HB 14-oz. tumblers. $30-40; $10-20 each

Blue pitcher and tumblers. $25-35; $10-15 each

Blenko Tangerine #361P 7" pitcher with #418L 8" tumblers. $35-45; $15-25 each

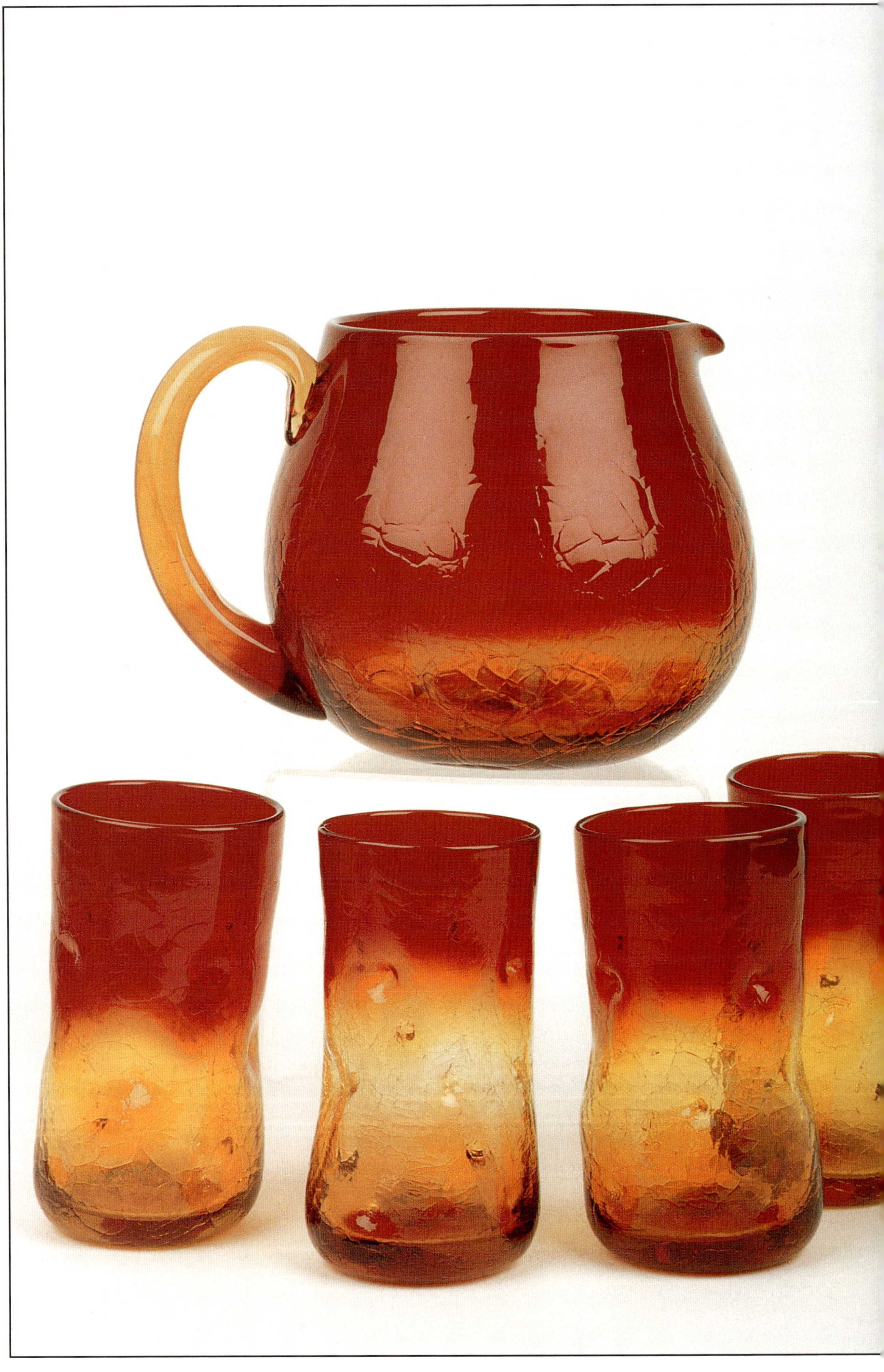

Pilgrim #47 Ruby 2-qt., 9" pitcher with #613W 10-oz. tumblers.
$35-45; $10-20 each

Blenko Crystal with Amethyst trim #445P 9-1/2" pitcher and #4450F 3-1/2" glasses with applied rosettes, or raspberry prunts. $40-60; $25-35 each

Blenko #445FB Crystal finger bowls with applied Sea Green raspberries. 4-1/4" d. $25-35 each

Two amber sugar and cream sets attributed to Hamon. Average 2-1/2" h. $20-30 set

Bischoff #400 Gold sugar and cream set. 3-1/2" h. $20-30 set

Kanawha #31 and #43 amberina sugar and cream sets. Average 3" h. $20-25 set

Below: Blenko miniature #C60E sugar and #C60F cream sets in Sea Green and Tangerine. $30-40 set

Bottom: Pilgrim #109SC sugar and cream sets in Blue, Olive Green, and Crystal; with #754SC in Blue. 3-1/2" h. $20-30 set

Blenko Crystal mugs with Cobalt handles. 4-1/2" h. $20-25 each

Blenko Crystal sugar and cream set. Average 5" h. $30-40 set

Crystal 3-1/2" sugar and cream set and 5" vase with applied rigaree, attributed to Hamon. $20-25 set; $10-15

Pilgrim #900 Blue 8" candy jar. $50-60

Two Blenko #7228L Ruby canisters with cork tops. 8-1/2" h. $20-30 each

Blenko #629M Turquoise 8-1/2" compote and #629S Olive Green and Tangerine 6" compotes. $40-50; $25-35

Pilgrim #33 Tangerine 6" and #34 Lemon-Lime and Blue 9" brandy snifters. $25-35; $40-50

Pilgrim Amethyst #764 5" pitcher and #43 candy server. 7" d. $10-15 and $20-25

Kanawha #22 blue 6-1/2" salt and pepper set with similar 4" set. $20-30 set

Blenko #413L Crystal 13" goblet with Cobalt stem and #413 Crystal 8" goblet with Turquoise stem. $50-60; $40-50

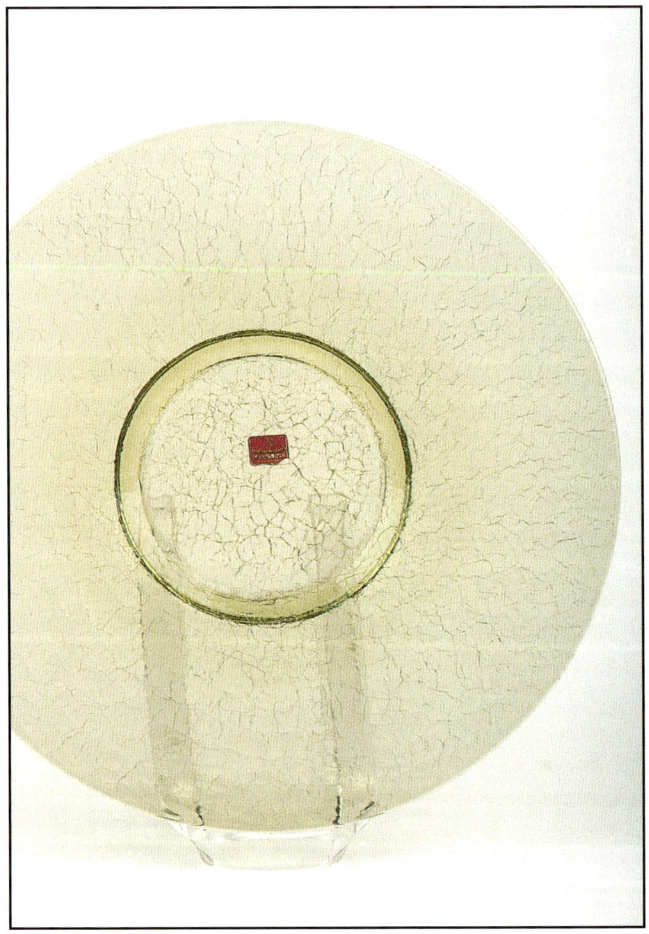

Viking Vaseline 15" platter. $40-60

Chapter 5: Bowls & Baskets

Footed bowls attributed to Bischoff. $15-25 each

Pilgrim #59S 6". Tangerine and Amethyst bowls and #59L 10" bowls in Crystal and Sky Blue. $15-20; $30-40

Pilgrim bowls:
#68 Tangerine 9". $30-40
#58L Ruby 12". $40-#58S Topaz 7". $15-20

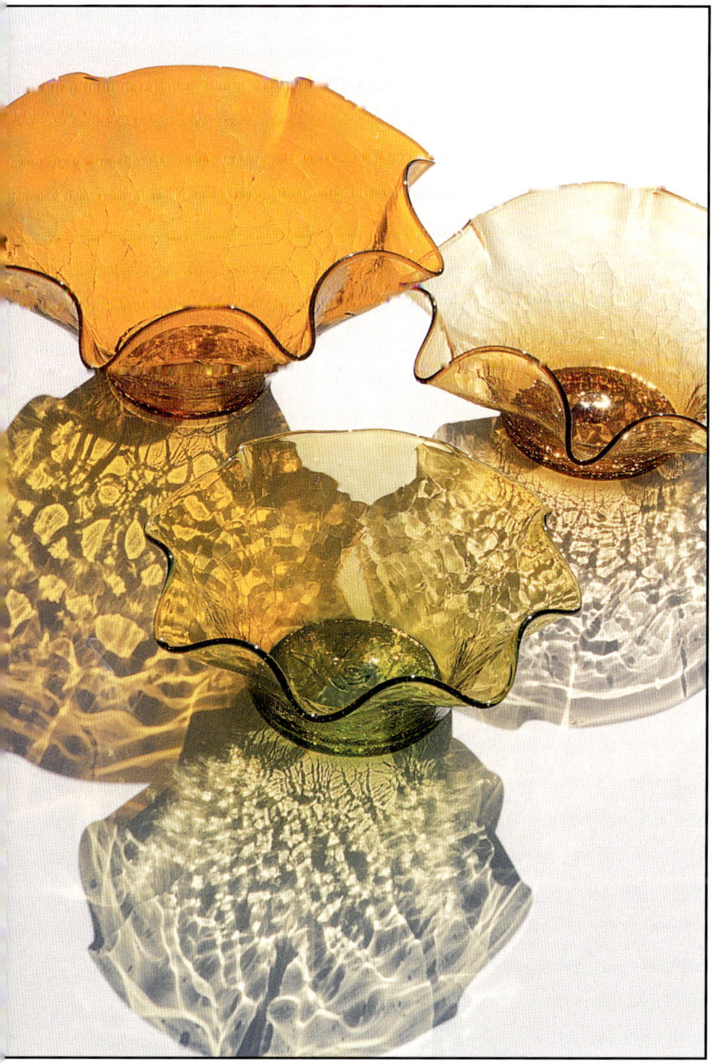

Bowls attributed to Bischoff. 5"-7" h. $25-40 each

Blenko #3744X 7" Turquoise and #3616 11" Turquoise and Sea Green bowls. $30-40; $50-60 each

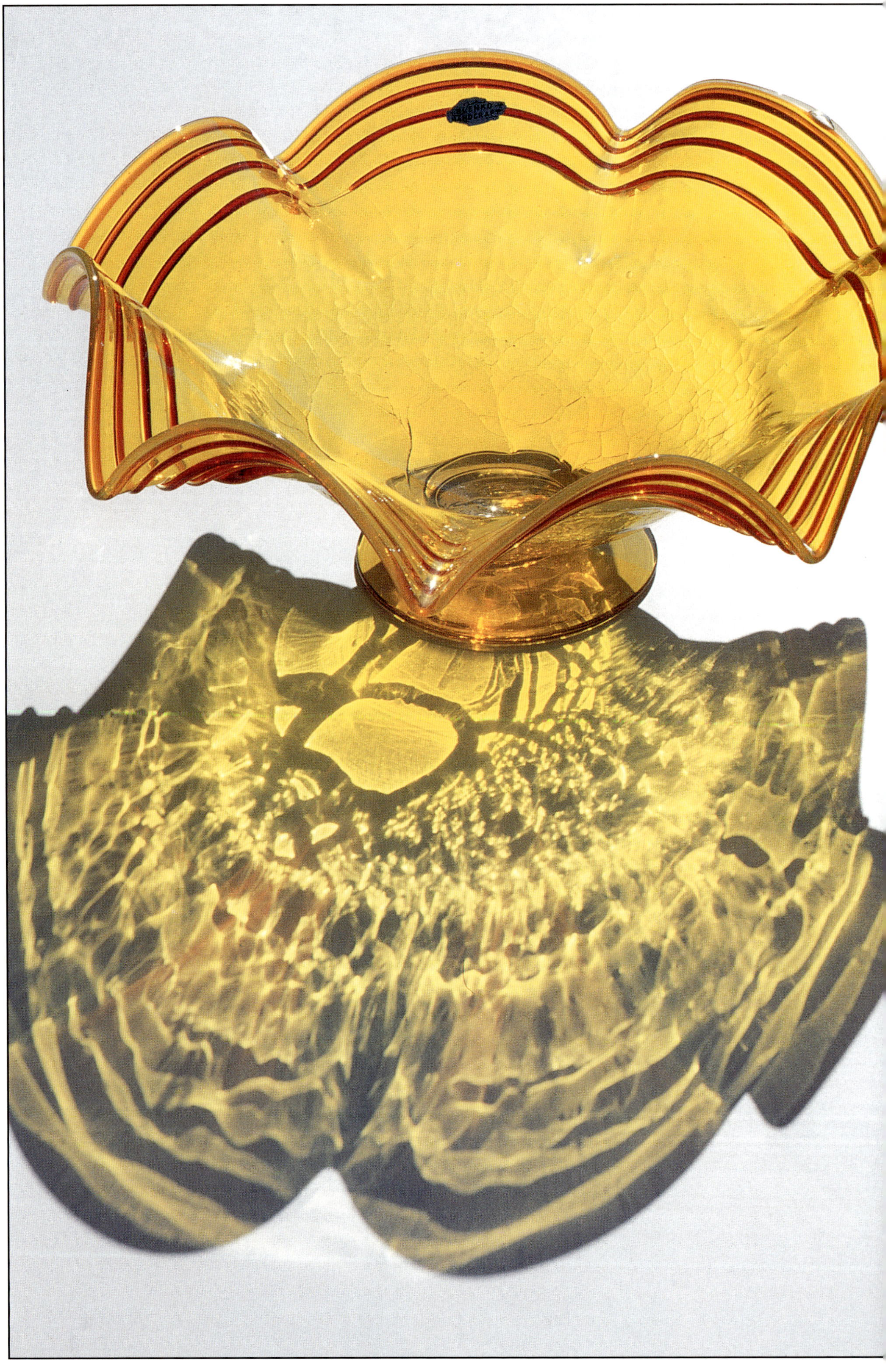

Blenko #6840 Jonquil with Ruby trim, designed by Joel Myers. 15-1/2" d. $60-80

Blenko #689 Jonquil 6" vase and ruffled bowls attributed to Blenko. $30-45 each

Two bowls and a vase attributed to Bischoff. $20-25 each

Rainbow small Amberina and larger Olive Green bowls. $15-20; $30-40

Opposite page:
Kanawha # 1110 amber and ruby 5-1/2" ivy bowls. $20-25
Blenko (attributed) Sea Green crimped bowl. $25-30
Blenko #538 Amethyst 4" crimped bowl. $30-40

Kanawha

Pilgrim #60 Emerald Green and Amethyst 5" crimped vases and #71 Topaz 7" crimped vase. $20-30; $40-50

Small Blenko bowls. $20-25 each

Blenko #7028 Amberina footed bowl. 11" d. $30-40
Blenko #30 shallow bowl with rolled rim. 12-1/2" d. $40-50

Three ruffled bowls and a footed fruit bowl attributed to Bischoff. $20-30 each

Pilgrim #44 Sky Blue, Tangerine, and Emerald Green footed bowls. 8" d. $25-35 each

Bischoff #435 Amberina bowl. 11-1/2" d. $50-60

Opposite page, top to bottom:
Pilgrim Sky Blue. $25-35 each:
#36 footed 5" bowl.
#32 chalice. 7" h.
#44 footed bowl. 8" d.

Two marigold bowls and a marigold basket. $20-30 each

Two unidentified cranberry flashed vases with a ruffled bowl by Blue Del. $25-35 each

Bischoff ruffled bowls:
#263 (top, vase) in Amethyst 8-1/4" h. $25-35
#505 Gold 4" bowl. $10-15
#506 Lemon 5" bowl. $15-20
#507 Lemon and Amethyst bowls. 8-1/2" d. $25-35 each

Bischoff label.

Green and Amberina footed bowls, possibly Bischoff. 5-1/2" d. $15-20 each

Footed bowls. $35-45 each
Kanawha #1050 blue footed bowl. 10-1/2" d.
Green Kanawha footed bowl. 11-1/2" d.
Bischoff Amberina 12" bowl.

Peacock Blue and Gold footed bowls attributed to Bischoff. $25-35 each

Footed bowls: Amberina, possibly Bischoff, and Kanawha #1050 blue. 10-1/2" d. $35-45 each

Blenko #420 crimped 7" bowl in Jonquil, with Bischoff copy in Poinsettia Red. $25-35; $15-25

Bischoff 6" handkerchief vases: #975 Poinsettia Red and #714 Emerald Green. $15-25 each

KANAWHA
KANAWHA
KANAWHA

Blenko Turquoise #6950 footed bowl. 7-3/4" d. $30-40

Bischoff 7" Gold copy of Blenko. $20-30

Blenko #9811L Crystal bowl with Cobalt trim. 11-1/2" d. $40-60

Opposite page, top to bottom:
Blue Del emerald green 5" bowl, with Bischoff 7" Green, 5" Poinsettia Red, and #505 Amberina ruffled bowls. $15-20 each

Group of small ruffled bowls attributed to Kanawha. $10-20 each

Top left: Blenko Crystal with Sea Green rosettes: 445LB (large bowl) 15" d. $80-100 (shown with small one)

Top right: Blenko Crystal bowls with Sea Green rosettes.

Blenko #445SB (small bowl) in Crystal with Sky Blue rosettes. 11" d. $50-70 (shown with small one)

Blenko #468L footed bowl in Crystal with Turquoise foot. 13" d. $70-90

Pilgrim Group LB miniature baskets in two shapes. Average 4-1/2" h. $15-20 each

Kanawha 5-1/2" baskets: #405 ruby and amberina, and #408 blue and yellow. $20-25 each

Group of baskets with similar handles possibly by Rainbow and Hamon.

Top left: Rainbow large Amberina basket with tag. 8-1/2" h. $40-50

Top right: Kanawha #273 blue and amberina 4" baskets, with 7" amberina. $15-20 each

Bottom left: Kanawha #1130, 1128, and 1131 ruby 5" baskets. $15-20 each:

Bottom right: Gibson blue basket. 8-1/2" h. $20-25

Chapter 6: Lighting & Figurals

Blenko Amethyst 6" candle holders. $50-70 pair

Bischoff #928 Amethyst 3" candle holders. $25-35 pair

Rainbow #712 Green 4" candle holders. $30-35 pair

Blenko #990 Jonquil 14" candle shades over #990A 3" candle holders. $40-50 each; $10-15 each

Kanawha #95 17" amberina and blue, with #94 11" green hurricanes. $40-50 each

Kanawha #106 blue 10-1/2" lamp with #93 green and amberina 11" hurricanes. $30-40 each

Rainbow #704 Olive Green 6" candle holders. $35-45 pair

Pilgrim #105 Tangerine 11" (rare) and #108 Blue 4" candle holders. $60-90 pair; $30-40 pair

Pair of 6" Tangerine whimsey candle holders, possibly Pilgrim. $35-45 pair

Rainbow fish. $50-80 each:
#9787 Tangerina, Amber, and Amberina. 12" l.
#D861 Ruby-Orange (duo-tone). 15" l.
#863 Green. 9" h.
Ruby 8" l. attributed to Rainbow.

Blenko #971M fish vases:
Antique Green and Crystal (1997). 16" l. $40-60
Olive Green (early). 17" l. $70-80

Blenko fish vases:
#5433 Amber. 10" h. $75-100
#971S Olive Green. 12-1/2" l. $50-60

Pilgrim #4 Smoke 11" Lucerne Fish. $50-70 Pilgrim #5 Blue 6" Swan. $20-25

Crystal fish with Green fins attributed to Rainbow. 8" l. $40-50

Pilgrim #4 Lucerne fish in Crystal and Crystal with Tangerine. $50-70 each

Kanawha swan bowls:

- #719 amberina and crystal. 9-1/2" l. $30-40
- #1162 ruby and crystal. 6" l. $20-25
- #1165 blue. 6-1/2" l. $20-25

Blenko #964 horn vase, designed by Winslow Anderson c. 1950:
Large Tangerine, 22" l, $125-150
Small Rosé, 18 1/2" l, $75-100

Blenko hats in black-amethyst and green and gold. $40-60; $20-30

A group of apples and pears. Some companies represented include Blenko, Hamon, and Rainbow. $30-60 each.

Large amethyst 11" eggplant and various pears by Blenko, Viking, and Rainbow. $40-60; $20-35 each

Various apples by Rainbow, Viking, and Kanawha. $30-60 each

Group of apples from Blenko, Hamon, and Kanawha. $30-60 each

Group of apples from Rainbow, Viking, and Kanawha. $20-25 each

Group of pastel colored apples, possibly by Blenko and Kanawha. $20-25 each

Labeled fruit by Viking, Rainbow, and Kanawha. $20-25 each

Orange with unsealed crackle which feels rough. $25-35

Bibliography

Adkins, Carl. "Roberto Moretti: Carver of Crystal." Typescript.

Alford, Judy. *Collecting Crackle Glass*. Atglen, Pennsylvania: Schiffer, 1995.

Corning Museum of Glass. *Glass 1959.* Corning, New York: Corning Museum, 1959.

———*New Glass: A Worldwide Survey.* Corning, New York, Corning Museum, 1979.

"Crackle Glass Heating Up." *Antique Trader's Collector Magazine* (Sept 1996): 7.

"Dalzell–Viking." *The Daze* (May 1992): 9.

Eige, Eason & Rick Wilson. *Blenko Glass: 1930–1953.* Marietta, Ohio: Antique Publications, 1987.

Eige, Eason. *A Century of Glassmaking in West Virginia.* Huntington, West Virginia: Huntington Galleries, 1980.

———"Pilgrim's New Cameo Glass." *Glass Collector's Digest* 4 (Oct/Nov 1990):31–37.

Fossell, Eric. "Glass Shop Thrives in Its Fragile Niche." *The Herald Dispatch.* [2000].

Garmon, Lee. "Dalzell–Viking: A Tradition Continues." *Glass Collector's Digest 3* (Dec/Jan 1990): 30–35.

Grayson, June. "Crackle Glass." *Glass Collector's Digest* (Oct/Nov 1989): 50–55.

McKeand, Robert. "A Brief History of the Pilgrim Glass Corporation, Ceredo, West Virginia." Typescript, 1986.

McKeand, Robert & Thomas O'Connor. "A Formula for Success: The Pilgrim Glass Story." *Glass Collector's Digest*. (June/July 1992): 35–42.

Miller, Everett R. & Addie R. *The New Martinsville Glass Story.* Marietta, Ohio: Richardson, 1972.

———*The New Martinsville Glass Story, Book II 1920–1950.* privately printed, 1975.

Piña, Leslie. *Fifties Glass.* Atglen, Pennsylvania: Schiffer, 1993.

——— *Blenko Glass 1962–1971 Catalogs* . Atglen, Pennsylvania: Schiffer, 2000.

——— *Blenko: Cool '50s & '60 Glass*. Atglen, Pennsylvania: Schiffer, 2000.

——— *Crackle Glass in Color: Depression to '70s.* Atglen, Pennsylvania: Schiffer, 2000.

——— *Blenko 1972–1983 Catalogs*. Atglen, Pennsylvania: Schiffer, 2001.

"Renowned glass craftsman Roberto Moretti dies at 57." *The Herald Dispatch.* (1986): A1–2.

Rhoads, Betty. "Kanawha Glass." *Glass Collector's Digest 3* (Feb/Mar 1990): 43–46.

Six, Dean. "Index to Encyclopedia of Wist Virginia Glass." Typescript, 1993.

———"Kanawha Peachblow." *Glass Collector's Digest* 6 (Oct/Nov 1992): 35–38.

Sutter, Sharon Hollis. "Dalzell–Viking: Tradition Looks to the Future." *A & E Business.* (Jan/Feb 1991): 6, 8, & 15.

Viking Glass Company. *Beauty is Glass from Viking.* New Martinsville, West Virginia: Viking Glass, 1967.

Welch, Lee Ann. "Glass collector keeping past alive." *The Wayne County News* (Dec. 1, 1993):3A.

West Virginia Department of Labor. *Directory of West Virginia Business and Industry.* Charleston, WV, 1950.

Wilson, Rick. "We're In For It: Early Days at Blenko Glass." *Goldenseal: West Virginia Traditional Life* 13 (Fall 1987): 43–49.

-------"Blenko Glass: An Inside Story." *Glass Collector's Digest* 1 (Oct/Nov 1987): 73–82.

———"Winslow Anderson." *Glass Collector's Digest* 2 (June/July 1988): 26–33.

Witek, John & Deborah Novak. *Hearts of Glass: the Story of Blenko Handcraft.* Video. Witek & Novak, Inc. for West Virginia Public Television, 1998.

Index

Adams, Hank, 8
Anderson, Winslow, 5, 8, 17, 19, 22, 59, 69, 151

Bischoff, 9, 25, 26, 36, 53, 56, 62, 69, 70, 73-75, 80, 84-89, 91, 117, 123, 125, 128, 131, 132, 134-137, 139, 143
Bischoff, Anthony F., 9
Bischoff, label, 134
Blenko, 7, 8, 16-23, 37, 40, 44, 59, 63-65, 67-69, 71, 73-80, 86-88, 90, 92-96, 99, 101, 102, 107-110, 114, 116, 118-122, 125-127, 130, 131, 137, 139, 140, 143, 144, 148, 151-155
Blenko, label, 7
Blenko, William H. (Bill), 8
Blenko, William John, 8
Blue Del, 10, 45, 48, 134, 138

Carter, Matt, 8, 76
Cummings, G.R., 14

Dalzell, Kenneth, 14
Desmeules, John, 10

Gibbons, Chris, 8
Gibson, 10, 52, 111, 142
Gibson, Charles, 10
Gibson, Phillip, 10
Gibson, Sharolyn Scites, 10
Goudeket, Joseph, 13

Hamon, 10, 29, 47, 48, 95, 105, 117, 119, 141, 152, 154
Hamon, Robert, 10
Heritage, 10
Husted, Wayne, 5, 6, 8, 9, 18-23, 37, 40, 67, 87, 88

Jamestown, 105

Kanawha, 10, 25, 29, 50, 58, 63, 67, 72, 81, 82, 92, 97-99, 101, 102, 105, 106, 109, 118, 122, 129, 135, 136, 138, 141, 142, 144, 145, 150, 154-156
Knobler, Alfred E., 12
Konrad, Karel, 12

Manus, Henry, 13
Meritt, D.P., 10
Miller, Elmer E., 14
Moretti, Alessandro, 5, 12
Moretti, Roberto, 5, 12
Muller, Axel, 8
Muller, Louis, 8
Myers, Joel, 5, 8, 20-22, 37, 44, 126

Nickerson, John, 8, 67

Pilgrim, 12, 19, 30, 34, 36, 47, 49, 57-60, 66, 69, 74, 83, 84, 87, 89, 90, 94, 103, 104, 109, 112, 113, 115, 118, 120-122, 124, 130, 132, 133, 141, 146, 147, 149, 150

Rainbow, 13, 16, 24, 26-29, 31-33, 35-43, 45-51, 54-56, 61, 62, 64, 70, 72, 83, 94, 96-100, 102, 128, 141-143, 145, 149, 152-156

Sandon, Mario, 12
Shepherd, Don, 8
Sponsler, Kathy, 10

Viking, 14, 68, 96, 122, 153-156

circa Fifties Glass from Europe & America
Leslie Piña

Here is the Italian and Scandinavian designer art glass usually referred to as "Fifties glass," plus a more popular modern glassware produced in factories, especially in the United States and Italy. This colorful and highly collectible glass is presented with detailed information on 88 designers and makers, design lists for Barovier & Toso and for Venini, glossary, bibliography, and index.

Size: 8 1/2" x 11" 505 photos 216 pp.
Value Guide/Index
ISBN: 0-7643-0229-9 hard cover $49.95

Depression Era Art Deco Glass
Leslie Piña

Explore American companies which made Art Deco glass during the Depression era: Cambridge, Consolidated, Duncan, Fostoria, Heisey, Libbey, Morgantown, Tiffin, and many others. With more than 350 color photos of popular and rare examples, informative captions with values, patent drawings, company information, a bibliography, and detailed index, this work will delight glass enthusiasts.

Size: 8 1/2" x 11" 342 color slides, 49 b & w diagrams
price guide, index 160 pp.
ISBN: 0-7643-0718-5 hard cover $24.95

Fostoria Designer George Sakier
Leslie Piña

For over fifty years Goerge Sakier sent classic and modern designs to Moundsville, West Virginia, where millions of delightful glass objects were produced. The book includes a thoroughly researched text about the man and his art (paintings, industrial designs and glass), color photos of thousands of Fostoria glass items of many patterns and Sakier's fascinating oil painting landscapes.

Size: 8 1/2" x 11" 380+ photos 176 pp.
Price Guide
ISBN: 0-88740-858-3 hard cover $29.95

Fostoria American Line 2056
Leslie Piña

Fostoria glass pattern "American No. 2056" has been a favorite of glass collectors. More than 400 color photographs and many black and white illustrations, detailed captions, a value guide, quick reference section, and an index will fascinate and inform dealers and collectors alike.

Size: 8 1/2" x 11" 379 color, 50 diagrams, 6 catalog pgs
Price Guide/Index 160 pp.
ISBN: 0-7643-0829-7 hard cover $29.95

Tiffin Glass, 1914-1940
Leslie Piña

Tiffin was one of the giants of American glassmaking. This is the first book to present all color photos of hundreds of Tiffin's products. Vases, bowls, and candlesticks in a wide variety of colors and styles, from common to rare, are all in this book, with large sections devoted to Tiffin's pressed satin glass, lamps, and baskets.

Size: 8 1/2" x 11" 527 color photos
Price Guide/Index 160 pp.
ISBN: 0-7643-0102-0 hard cover $29.95

Fostoria
Serving the American Table 1887-1986
Leslie Piña

A celebration of 100 years of American Fostoria glass, including rarely seen Victorian pattern glass from the early years in Fostoria, Ohio, through the introduction of color, the popular American and Coin patterns, and scarce and unusual, even unique, items. The book contains labels, color catalog pages, an illustrated styles chart with over 1000 entries, a chronology, index, and a price guide.

Size: 8 1/2" x 11" 400+ color photos 192 pp.
Price Guide/Index
ISBN: 0-88740-726-9 hard cover $29.95

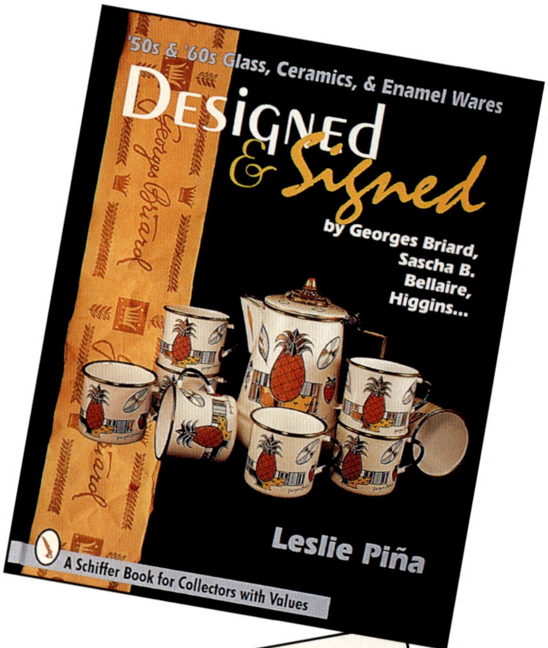

Designed & Signed

'50s & '60s Glass, Ceramics & Enamel Wares by Georges Briard, Sascha Brastoff, Marc Bellaire, Higgins

Leslie Piña

Highly collectible household objects designed and signed by name artists of the 1950s and 1960s are presented here including gift and tableware, glass, ceramics and enamel items. Much is written about the leading designer and marketing wizard Georges Briard, and many of his designs are pictured, along with much work by the other prominent featured artists

Size: 8 1/2 x 11" 587 color photos 192 p

Price Guide

ISBN: 0-88740-935-0 hard cover $29.9

Fifties Glass

Revised and Expanded 2nd Edition

Leslie Piña

Special emphasis is given to Italian (Murano) and Scandinavian glass, with artist and designer biographies, company histories, an illustrated glossary, an illustrated section on signatures and labels, index, and a price guide. Ranging from common collectibles to museum quality art, these glass objects from the 1950s are all within that range of style, color, quality, and fun that we now identify as "fifties glass."

Size: 8 1/2" x 11" 381 photos 208 p

Price Guide/Index

ISBN: 0-7643-0986-2 hard cover $49.9

Blenko Glass

1962-1971 Catalogs

Leslie Piña

First begun in the late nineteenth century in Milton, West Virginia, Blenko remains one of the few glass factorie in the United States where modern hand blown glass is still in production. Recently, Blenko glass designs fro the 1950s and 1960s have caught collectors' eyes. This book presents an exact, full-color reprinting of the yearly Blenko company catalogs from 1962 through 1971, thus offering a complete, well-illustrated record of Blenko glass products, including original retail prices and up-to-date prices.

Size: 8 1/2" x 11" 180 color photos 160 p

Price Guide

ISBN: 0-7643-1026-7 hard cover $29.9

Depression Era Glass by Duncan

Leslie Piña

Glassware made by The Duncan & Miller Glass Company, of Washington, Pennsylvania, in the 1920s -1940s featured. This book presents their Depression Era production and includes essays about their Victorian wares and contribution to the Tiffin Glass Co. Over 500 color photos, catalog pages, advertisements, patent drawings, chronology of company history, detailed captions, bibliography, index, and value guide make this a complete reference for the popular glassware.

Size: 11" x 8 1/2" 457 color photos, 82 b/w images 176 p

Price Guide/Index

ISBN: 0-7643-0928-5 hard cover $29.9

HAND BLOWN BY
Rainbow
HUNTINGTON, W. VA.
U.S.A.